SPLIT

AN UPDATED TRAVEL GUIDE

Uncover the City's Best-Kept Secrets:
Your Guide to a Smooth and Enjoyable
Trip.

John Schnell

TABLE OF CONTENTS

INTRODUCTION

As soon as I stepped off the boat into Split's sun-kissed shoreline, the city's unique mix of history and contemporary captured my attention. This Croatian seaside jewel had long been on my bucket list as a wanderer with an insatiable want to explore, and now I was finally experiencing its rich tapestry.

The ancient Diocletian's Palace is without a doubt the beating heart of Split. It seemed as if time had stood still as you passed past its old walls. The stone walkways, polished by decades of foot use, reverberated with distant echoes. I explored the Palace's secret courtyards decorated with vivid bougainvillea and little eateries that appeared to erupt from the building's very core as I meandered through its tiny pathways. The Peristyle, the palace's main courtyard, was a magnificent sight. Emperor Diocletian sent the Egyptian sphinx as a gift, and it served as a sentinel to watch over the tales inscribed on the marble columns.

Split is a dynamic, breathing city, not merely a remnant of the past. That was shown by the lively Riva promenade that ran along the shore. The coastline came alive as the sun set with residents and tourists alike walking, enjoying gelato, and drinking coffee. Laughter and the mouthwatering smells of seafood from the adjacent eateries filled the air. I found a position on the stairs next to the statue of Gregory of Nin, marveled at its enormous figure, and stroked its sparkling toe like many others before me for luck.

I took a tour of the bustling Green Market to get a feel for local life. The stalls had abundant bright fruits, veggies, cheeses, and crafts. I learned about the renowned Dalmatian culinary traditions from the merchants. The locally produced tomatoes' vivid red color appeared to represent the community's love for its food.

Marjan Hill was one of the highlights of my trip. Panoramas of the city and the Adriatic Sea were the rewards for the climb. I settled into a peaceful position at the top and looked out over the ethereal blue seas. Church bells ringing in the distance and the faint laughter of kids playing on the beaches below could be heard on the calm wind. I was really delighted when the sun started to set and produced a lovely golden glow.

I couldn't pass up the chance to visit Split's Archaeological Museum since it was filled with historical items that helped me better comprehend Split's turbulent past. Ancient sculptures, beautiful ceramics, and elaborate mosaics all helped to portray a vivid image of the life that once flourished within the Diocletian's Palace.

Without enjoying Dalmatian food, my trip would not have been complete. I went inside a cute konoba that was hidden away in the maze of streets. The air was filled with the smells of grilled fish and flavorful meats. I tucked into a meal of fresh fish and a bottle of local wine, savoring the symphony of tastes that reflected the abundance of the Adriatic.

As my stay in Split drew to a close, I started to understand that this city had provided me with more than simply stunning scenery. It created a unique tapestry of experiences by weaving the threads of antiquity and modernity together. I was forever changed by Split's warmth, the kind smiles of its inhabitants, and the tangible sense of its connection to its past. Even though I was leaving Split physically as I got on the boat, I knew that a part of me would always be within its storied walls and sunny shoreline.

WELCOME TO SPLIT

Location and Geography

One of Croatia's biggest and most beautiful cities, Split is situated on a magnificent semi-island in the Dalmatian area. The city was founded in the third century and is one of the oldest in the Adriatic Sea area. With wonderful historic architecture, museums, galleries, top-notch hotels, restaurants, and a ton of shopping centers and art galleries, it is one of the most alluring and intriguing tourist destinations in the area.

On the Split (Marjan) peninsula, Split is located in the heart of Dalmatia. Split, a peninsula encircled by the sea, is also bordered by the nearby mountains of Mosor to the northeast and Kozjak to the northwest. Marjan Hill, one of the city's most significant emblems, rises on the peninsula's west side, just outside the ancient city center. Bra, Hvar, Olta, and Iovo are the other islands that encircle Split.

Split is the main city in Dalmatia and the second-largest city in Croatia, with about 180.000 residents as of the most recent census, which was held in 2011. One of the biggest passenger harbors in the Mediterranean, but the second-largest freight harbor in Croatia. It serves as the county's administrative hub for Split and Dalmatia.

History

Split's long history is a narrative of development, change, and the lingering impact of several civilizations that have defined its identity. Split, located in Croatia on the eastern bank of the Adriatic Sea, has a long history.

The Roman Emperor Diocletian is credited with founding the city when he chose the location for an opulent retirement residence at the beginning of the fourth century AD. The Diocletian royal complex served as the foundation upon which Split progressively grew. The palace was a wonder of architecture, with elaborate masonry, grand gateways, and opulent chambers. A military garrison, a combination of residential and commercial rooms, and even a mausoleum—which subsequently evolved into the Cathedral of St. Domnius—were all situated inside the palace.

Split saw several difficulties and invasions from different peoples, notably Goths, Avars, and Slavs, as the Roman Empire withered. By the seventh century, the city was ruled by the Byzantines and developed into a prominent commercial and cultural hub for the area. One of the world's earliest Christian churches, the Cathedral of St. Domnius represents the city's long Christian tradition. It was dedicated in the seventh century.

Split eventually joined the medieval Croatian Kingdom and, in the 15th century, fell under the influence of the Venetians. Palaces, churches, and public spaces demonstrate the Venetians' distinctive architectural influence on the city.

Split found itself on the front lines of the battle between the Ottoman Turks and the Venetians in the 16th century as a result of the Ottoman Empire's expansion into the area. Defensive fortifications and buildings, such as the Fortress of Klis, erected by the Venetians and perched on a neighboring hill overlooking the city, were common during this time.

Split joined the Austro-Hungarian Empire in the 19th century, and urban growth led to urbanization and industry. The port of the city grew in significance as a center for marine connection and commerce, further forming its economic and cultural character.

More substantial alterations emerged in the 20th century. Split was absorbed into the newly created Kingdom of Serbs, Croats, and Slovenes after World War I, which subsequently evolved into Yugoslavia. The Italians first occupied the city during World War II, then the Germans. Split was a member of the Socialist Federal Republic of Yugoslavia during the post-war era, which was governed by Josip Broz Tito.

Croatia claimed independence when Yugoslavia broke apart in the early 1990s, which started the Croatian War of Independence. Split, which is in the south of the nation, suffered little during the battle and has since developed into a major cultural, economic, and tourist hub.

The history of Split is still evident wherever you look today. Its focal point, the Diocletian's Palace, is still there; it is a UNESCO World Heritage Site and a bustling urban complex where the past and present coexist. Visitors come from all over the globe to the city's picturesque old town, busy waterfront, and dynamic cultural scene to take in the many facets of history that have shaped this magnificent Croatian jewel.

Culture and People

Split's residents, known as "Splicani" in Croatian, have unique qualities that set them apart from other Croatians.

In general, they are very funny, friendly, sometimes haughty and arrogant, but above all, they are tremendously proud of their city. People in their city will claim that it is "the most beautiful city in the world and beyond."

It is stated that they are lethargic, but the sloth is more tied to certain climatic conditions and a state of mind and body known as "fjaka," which is when a guy lacks the will to accomplish anything.

The Dalmatian idea of "fjaka" represents a relaxed style of life that emphasizes contentment and relaxation. Locals often congregate along the Riva promenade where they engage in animated discussion and people-watch. The community's strong social ties provide a friendly environment for both locals and guests.

The "Splicani" have a strong dedication to sports including football, water polo, tennis, basketball, athletics, rowing, and swimming. They also like singing, fine dining, and wine.

Their hometown and the neighborhood football (soccer) team, Hajduk, are two things they are most proud of. Poljud Stadium has been referred to as "the stadium with the best atmosphere in Europe" and Hajduk is one of the clubs with the highest fan support in the nation.

The city of immigrants is Split. 49.7% of immigrants in 2002, according to studies, came from the hinterland of Dalmatia, 10.2% from the island, 8.5% from Split's coastal cities, 9% from Bosnia and Herzegovina, 16.2% from other regions of Croatia, and 6.4% from other sources.

The Croatian language is essential to Split's culture, and its speakers take great pleasure in maintaining their dialect. Although it may be pleasantly difficult for visitors to comprehend, the distinctive Dalmatian accent captures the essence of the city. Language preservation and cultural heritage preservation go hand in hand.

The majority of the population consists of Croat residents. Gypsies, Hungarians, and Serbs are among the minorities. Roman Catholicism predominates, although there are also Orthodox Christian, Muslim, and Jewish minorities.

Weather and Climate

In accordance with the Köppen-Geiger classification, Split experiences a moderate oceanic climate, including warm summers.

The yearly average maximum temperature in Split is 19°C (ranging from 10°C in January to 30°C in August). Annual rainfall is 1130mm, with a minimum of 30mm in August and a maximum of 156mm in November.

Between January and February, the climate is unfavorable. The record temperature this month is 17°C and, in February, 6 days of rain are expected.

During the month of March, the climate is appropriate. By early evening, the temperature averages 10°C and you can expect to have 92mm of rainfall/month during this period.

The climate is pleasant from April to June.

The temperature rises to 26°C and it rains in June about 74mm.

The climate is highly favorable during the period from July to August. The temperature rises to 30°C and it rains about 4% of the time in August.

During the months of September and October, the climate is favorable. At lunchtime, it's 20°C on average and it rains in October about 100mm.

In the month of November, the climate is not good, but still OK. It is for example 16°C as maximum temperature in November and it rains in November about 156mm.

During December, the climate is not favorable. The record temperature this month is 17°C and you can expect to have 127mm of rainfall/month during this period.

Current Security, Political and Social Situation

The current political, social, and security situation in Split is generally stable. Croatia is a member of the European Union and NATO, and the city is located in a relatively peaceful region. However, there are some potential security risks that should be considered before visiting Split.

One potential security risk is terrorism. Split is a popular tourist destination, and it could be a target for terrorist attacks.

Another potential security risk is crime. Petty crime, such as pickpocketing and bag snatching, is common in Split. Visitors should take steps to secure their goods and be alert of their surroundings.

The political situation in Croatia is also relatively stable. However, there is some political tension between Croatia and Serbia. This tension could potentially lead to security problems in Split.

Overall, the current political, social, and security situation in Split is generally stable. However, there are some potential security risks that should be considered before visiting the city.

FASCINATING THINGS THAT MAKE SPLIT AN INTERESTING DESTINATION

The World's Oldest Catholic Cathedral

The oldest Catholic cathedral in continuous use worldwide is the Cathedral of Saint Domnius, which was dedicated in the year 700. It was also the second-oldest building ever utilized by a Christian cathedral when it was constructed in 305 AD as the Mausoleum of Diocletian.

Where The Name Split Came From

When you see yellow flowers blooming in the hills around Split in the spring, it's more than simply the start of a warmer season. According to mythology, the flower, known in Croatian as brnistra and in English as Spanish broom or weaver's broom, is where the city's name originated.

Aspalathos, the name of the original Greek village that formerly stood on the same site before the Romans arrived, serves as a hint for the puzzle. The name of the current city was derived from Aspalathos through Spalatium, Spalatum, Spalato, and then Split.

The alternative hypothesis is much less romantic and seductively straightforward; as a result, the name was given after Diocletian's Palace had already been constructed, and the relationship is palatium (palace).

The late fourth-century classic Roman road map makes reference to Spalato. So, you may choose whatever version you like most. And even without it, those yellow blossoms are lovely!

Where the Last Legitimate Roman Emperor was Assassinated

The last legitimate emperor of the Western Roman Empire, Julius Nepos, was assassinated in the streets outside Diocletian's Palace on April 25, 480. His name is given to a street in Split, and one instance of how locals work to protect their history is via the creation of murals that include his life.

Romulus Augustulus, just 12 years old, overthrew Julius Nepos in 474 and took power until Julius Nepos escaped to

Dalmatia in 475. Romulus, however, was never acknowledged by Constantinople as their only legitimate ruler in the West; instead, they continued to accept Julius Nepos as such.

He remained the Emperor of Dalmatia until 480 when his own men assassinated him.

The City with the Most Number of Olympic Medalists Per Resident

Split is renowned for its athletes and athletic accomplishments. The Walk of Fame in Split honors its athletic greats, including Wimbledon champion Goran Ivanisevic, semi-religious sensation Hajduk, and more than seventy Olympic gold winners.

Aside from all of this, don't forget about one of my favorite sports trivia: local basketball team Jugoplastika was named the greatest team of the 20th century by FIBA. Yes, Split is the nation's sports capital.

The Third-Oldest Bookshop in Europe

Established in 1860 by Vid Morpurgo, the Morpurgo bookshop in Split is one of the oldest in all of Europe. Only in Paris and Lisbon can you locate older ones; it's on the main plaza. It underwent renovation a few years ago, and the old-style doors were reinstalled. Additionally, there is no worry that it will leave since this location is protected by local ordinance and the only permitted activity is the sale of books. The same is true with Karaman, Split's first movie theater, which opened in 1908!

An Egyptian sprinkling on the Mediterranean

The sphinx is, together with the pyramids, the most well-known representation of ancient Egypt and the legends surrounding it. However, did you know that Split, Croatia, has sphinxes right in the middle of it? What's the relationship between Split and Egypt?

Diocletian, the emperor who is credited for fortifying Split, was a huge admirer of Egyptian tradition. Furthermore, Egypt was a Roman province throughout his reign, making Emperor Diocletian the true "owner" of Egypt. As a result, he was able to take what he wanted without any trouble or expenditure.

He chose to bring sphinxes with him to adorn his vacation home in Split because he thought they were particularly beautiful. He purportedly gave the order for up to 12 sphinxes to be brought from Egypt to adorn the palace's exterior. Due to the notion that sphinxes were pagan emblems, the majority of them were demolished during Christian efforts.

The one on the Peristil, fashioned of black African granite and standing erect for countless years in one of Split's most lovely squares, is the best maintained. It dates back more than 3000 years to the reign of Pharaoh Thutmose III, making it one of the oldest topics in Split.

Split Sport, Picigin

It is vital to mention picigin [pitzigin] while discussing sports. Played by individuals of all ages, picigin is a Croatian amateur sport that was developed in Split, notably on Bavice Beach. It is recognized as part of Croatia's intangible cultural heritage. Even though picigin is primarily a summer activity, fans participate all year long, and playing on the first day of the new year in Bavice is already customary.

Since there are no victors in the game Picigin, it is difficult to discuss severe regulations. The fundamental principles are relatively straightforward: five players are situated in a pentagon six to seven meters apart in a sea that is ten to twenty centimeters deep (if the sea is deeper, it just slows down the game and makes it less exciting).

They utilize a ball, known as a "balun" in local parlance, beating it with their hands in an effort to keep it from falling into the water.

The slogan "go slowly," "little by little," and "no hurry" is fostered by Split, and this guiding idea is also sensed in the custom of drinking coffee for many hours.

In Split, going out for coffee is more than simply a routine that involves sipping coffee; it's also about engaging in social interaction and making new friends.

When you walk by the Riva in Split and see packed cafés, bear in mind that "coffee" is only a placeholder for the Mediterranean ritual of socializing that the people of Dalmatia love dearly. If you go "for coffee" with a local, it's likely that it won't be a quick encounter.

Islam's Prophet at a Franciscan Monastery

Only the Franciscan monastery in Split is home to one of the few known images of the prophet Muhammad. After discovering the picture of their prophet inside the Church in the 16th century, the Turks were about to burn and destroy both the Church and the monastery until they were halted by this image.

VISA REQUIREMENT

The laws and rules governing who is permitted to enter Croatia without a visa and who needs a visa to visit the country are outlined in the Croatian visa policy.

Since Croatia is a member of the European Union (EU), it adheres to the same visa regulations as the rest of the EU and grants visa-free travel to all EU nationals.

Croatia has visa-free arrangements with a number of foreign countries. The duration of a visa-free stay in Croatia is determined by the traveler's nationality.

To obtain access, visa-exempt people must merely display a passport valid for at least three months at Croatian border crossings.

All other foreign nationals must get a visa to enter Croatia, regardless of the duration of their stay or the purpose of the visit.

Because an eVisa or visa on arrival for Croatia is not presently available, individuals who want a visa must apply in person at the closest Croatian Embassy or Consulate.

The applicant must provide a variety of supporting documents before the travel document may be approved. These documents change depending on whether the applicant requires a Croatian visa for tourism, business, transit, job, or study, or for another reason.

To provide enough processing time, applicants should schedule an embassy visa appointment well in advance of their desired arrival date.

Tourist Visa

According to Croatia's tourist visa policy, residents of the EU have unrestricted mobility for tourism reasons, while other visa-free nationals are permitted a limited visa-free tourist stay, normally up to 90 days, depending on their country.

Other than the approximately 90 visa-exempt nationalities, all other foreign nationals must get a Croatian travel visa to enter the country, regardless of the length of stay or the reason for the visit.

According to Croatian visa regulations, tourists from around 150 countries need a visa to visit Croatia.

To apply for a tourist visa to Croatia, travelers must visit a Croatian government diplomatic office in their country of residence in person since an electronic visa or visa on arrival are not currently available.

This procedure entails presenting a completed Croatian tourist visa application form and a variety of supporting papers to an embassy interview, as well as paying a processing fee before the application can be accepted, which might take several weeks.

BEST TIME TO VISIT

The months of September and October are ideal for visiting Split since there are fewer tourists and the Adriatic Sea is still warm enough for swimming. The temperature often drops into the 40s and 50s by November and stays there for the remainder of the winter. The city's peak season is in July when the weather is hot and both visitor numbers and prices for lodging, flights, and rental vehicles are at their maximum. Temperatures and crowds increase from April through June.

September-October

The autumn months are a fantastic time to visit Split sans the summertime tourist hordes. Additionally, you may still spend some time at the beach due to the high average temperatures in the 60s and 70s. This time of year, water temperatures typically hover between the high 60s and the mid-70s.

November-March

The low season in Split is defined as the period from November to March. Travelers will find it too frigid to swim in the water with typical temperatures that fluctuate between the 40s and 50s, but they'll be pleasantly delighted by the cheaper lodging prices.

April-June

Another shoulder season in Split is from spring to early summer when hotel prices are beginning to climb and the number of visitors isn't at an all-time high. However, the weather is almost ideal: The water is comfortable for swimming with temperatures in the 60s and 70s, and average highs gradually increase from the 60s to the 70s.

July-August

Due to the large number of families traveling during school vacations, these months are considered Split's peak season, and as a result, hotel rates and temperatures are at all-time highs. Nevertheless, it's simple to see why so many visitors choose to come during this season: The typical sea temperature is in the mid-seventies, making it perfect for boat cruises and swimming.

SOME CULTURAL ETIQUETTE AND CUSTOMS TO KNOW

Being late is not considered impolite in Croatia, but simply spending 30 minutes with someone for coffee is. When extending a handshake in greeting, you're okay.

Punctuality: People in Croatia tend to be more laid back and on time. When someone asks you to meet them at 2:00 pm, they typically mean 2:15 pm or even a little later since things often run late.

In the workplace, things are a bit more "on time," but in daily life, individuals aren't too bothered by set schedules for meetings, departures, etc. It's not considered disrespectful in Croatia if someone is a little late to meet you, so don't take offense.

The phrase *"polako"* (which means slowly or slow down) is used a lot in Croatia. When you encourage someone to pick up the pace, they may exclaim "polako." Likewise, if they notice you rushing, they'll use the same term, *"polako."*

And when you declare your impending arrival, expect to hear the response "*samo polako*" from others. When you announce you're on your way, people will reply "*samo polako*" (just slowly). This term well captures Croatia's "punctuality" culture.

Croatians often dress quite beautifully and care about their appearance. Rarely will you encounter someone around town who is in disarray. Even for a carton of milk, people in this country wait until they are extremely well-presented (hair, makeup, and attire) before leaving the home.

Nonetheless, there exists a peculiar occurrence concerning sports and track pants as well as sweaters. Men may be seen all over town wearing many kinds of "sports attire," but I haven't yet seen a lady do the same. It's not unusual to see a guy in a tracksuit strolling beside a lady who is dressed for a formal dinner party.

Public transportation etiquette states that you should always give up your seat to an elderly or pregnant person while riding a bus or tram around the city.

In Croatia, there are many distinct methods to welcome people. It is rather tricky and relies on the other person's proximity to you as well as your gender.

1. Men nearly always shake hands when they meet one another, whether they are family members or complete strangers (although they sometimes give each other a double cheek kiss and a hug if they are really close friends).

2. If a man and woman are buddies, they will simultaneously kiss each other on the cheeks and shake hands. They will shake hands when they first meet if they are merely acquaintances.

3. Women give their female friends a kiss on each cheek and maybe an embrace, but they shake hands with strangers.

4. Typically, people only kiss youngsters on the head. When dealing with youngsters, there's no necessity for handshakes or exchanging double-cheek kisses, simplifying interactions.

Other Considerations with Regard to Greetings:

When you say hello and farewell to someone, you exchange the same words.

It's crucial to look the other person in the eye while shaking hands.

When in a group, men will always shake a woman's hand first.

There is no set order in which you kiss the first cheek while doing a double cheek kiss. If you both bend to the same side at once, you can wind up with a big ol' kiss on the lips. So just let the other person start and follow their lead.

The figures matter when it comes to kissing. The magic number is two (one kiss on each cheek). It will be strange if you kiss someone on one cheek only to draw back after they have already leaned in to kiss your other cheek.

Also, don't attempt to kiss three times. That's customary in the neighboring country of Serbia, so you'll be the uncomfortable one who leaned in as they drew away.

It might be awkward when one person goes in for the kiss while the other goes for the handshake.

My suggestion is to just extend your hand for a handshake, and if someone kisses you on both cheeks as you shake hands, just go through with it! However, a handshake will always keep you safe.

The bulk of socialization takes place over coffee. The two of you will either meet someplace in the city or will host or be hosted at a home where coffee will be "skuhati kavu" (cooked). You may bring a little present when you visit someone at home, but if it's a close friend whom you see often, a gift isn't really essential.

When you arrive at someone's home after being invited, they will always give you slippers. People will also anticipate that you'll have spare slippers for them if they come into your house, even if you're not required to wear them (although they'll be confused if you don't).

Every home has many pairs of "guest slippers," generally in various sizes.

You can escape the slipper problem if you meet for coffee in a café, but there will usually be a "fight" about who gets to pay at the conclusion of the meeting. When your gathering is over, someone will grab the receipt, and usually, the one who grabs the receipt first wins (and has to pay).

Upon accepting the receipt, the victor is entreated by the other individual to allow them to cover the expenses, but the winner declines the offer. People like treating their friends when they get together for coffee or a drink, so it's interesting to see this "receipt fight" every time.

Nevertheless, it's crucial to recognize that if you were the individual who took the initiative to arrange the gathering and extended the invitation to the other person, you do possess the advantage of being able to shoulder the expenses.

Honesty: Croatians are really honest people. They won't tell you something looks lovely if it doesn't, won't tell you something tastes delicious if it doesn't, and won't be shy about telling you if you've gained a few pounds over the holidays (that just means you had fun)!

Gifts: It's customary in Croatia to bring a modest gift when you are welcomed to someone's home. Nothing overly lavish, simply a bottle of wine, a bit of chocolate, or a pack of cookies will suffice. Here, it's also customary for the host to accept the present and open it right away (if it is wrapped or placed in a gift bag, of course).

Flowers are pleasant too, but they only bring an odd number; reportedly, an even number of flowers is only presented in cases of bereavement.

It's also customary to bring a modest present for the kids if you're visiting a family with young kids (this may be something basic like a Kinder Egg, some sweets, or a simple toy). **Kids like having visitors around since they often get a tiny treat:)**

SOME USEFUL PHRASES AND VOCABULARY TO UNDERSTAND

Let's dive into some useful Croatian phrases and vocabulary that will be incredibly handy during your visit to Split. Learning even a few basic phrases can greatly enhance your experience and interactions with locals. Here's a breakdown of essential language you might want to know:

Greetings and Basic Phrases:

Bok / Zdravo - Hello

Dobar dan - Good day

Dobro jutro - Good morning

Dobra večer - Good evening

Laku noć - Good night

Hvala - Thank you

Molim - Please

Izvinite - Excuse me / I'm sorry

Da - Yes

Ne – No

Introductions and Courtesy:

Kako se zovete? - What is your name?

Zovem se [Your Name]. - My name is [Your Name].

Drago mi je. - Nice to meet you.

Molim vas, ponovite. - Please repeat.

Molim vas, govori li tko engleski? - Does anyone speak English?

Basic Conversational Phrases:

Kako ste? - How are you?

Hvala, dobro. - Thank you, I'm good.

Koliko košta? - How much does it cost?

Imam rezervaciju. - I have a reservation.

Gdje je WC? - Where is the restroom?

Getting Around:

Gdje je...? - Where is...?

Gdje je hotel? - Where is the hotel?

Gdje je restoran? - Where is the restaurant?

Gdje je plaža? - Where is the beach?

Koliko košta karta? - How much is the ticket?

Jedna karta za [destination], molim. - One ticket to [destination], please.

Kako da dođem do...? - How do I get to...?

Eating and Drinking:

Jedno pivo, molim. - One beer, please.

Jedna kava, molim. - One coffee, please.

Jedna voda, molim. - One water, please.

Račun, molim. - The bill, please.

Jelovnik, molim. - The menu, please.

Imate li vegetarijanski jelovnik? - Do you have a vegetarian menu?

Emergency Phrases:

Pomoć! - Help!

Hitna pomoć - Emergency help

Policija - Police

Bolnica - Hospital

Gubi se! - Go away!

Polite Closing Phrases:

Doviđenja. - Goodbye.

Hvala na svemu. - Thank you for everything.

Lijep dan. - Have a nice day.

Laku noć. - Good night.

Remember, learning a few phrases shows respect for the local culture and often results in more positive interactions. Even if English is widely spoken, making an effort to communicate in Croatian can go a long way in connecting with locals and enhancing your overall experience in Split.

GETTING TO SPLIT

Due to its extensive transit network, getting to Split is rather simple. If you're coming from outside of Croatia or from another country, you have a few choices to consider:

By Air: The main international entry point into the city is Split Airport (Resnik Airport). The airport, which is about 24 kilometers (15 miles) west of the city center, provides a range of flights and serves several European locations. Once you've landed, it won't take you long to go to the city using a cab, shuttle, or public transit.

By Rail: You may still get to Split by rail, despite Croatia's small train network compared to other modes of transportation. A little beyond the city's core is where the railway station is situated. There are direct trains from significant cities like Zagreb, however, the trip may take several hours. Beautiful vistas may be seen throughout the road that follows the shore.

By Bus: In Croatia, buses are a common and practical means of transportation. Buses are available to take you from Split to numerous destinations in Croatia and adjacent nations. Near the city's heart and harbor lies Split Bus Station, the primary bus station. Buses provide pleasant transportation alternatives and are well-maintained.

By Ferry: Taking a ferry to Split is an excellent alternative if you're traveling from an island or close-by coastal city. Port of Split, the city's port, has excellent connections to the nearby islands of Bra, Hvar, Vis, and Korula. International ferries are also available from Italian cities including Pescara and Ancona.

By Vehicle: Renting a vehicle is a wonderful option if you value freedom and wish to explore the beautiful seaside road. From major Croatian towns like Zagreb or Dubrovnik, the travel is pleasurable and enables you to stop at lovely locations along the route. But pay attention to the flow of traffic and the state of the roads, particularly during the busiest travel times.

By Cruise Ship: When cruise ships are sailing along the Adriatic coast, Split is a common port of call. Split is often included in the itineraries of cruise ships, enabling travelers to quickly experience the city's top attractions. The city core is ideally close to the cruise terminal, making it simple to go about on foot.

TRAVELLING AROUND SPLIT

How to Navigate Split

The most convenient method to move about Split is by automobile since it allows you to choose your own schedule, but hiring a car isn't the most cost-effective option.

The money may be saved by relying on city buses (and ferries for island hopping). You can easily move about on foot, however, if you want to stay near to Old Town.

Many visitors use Split Airport (SPU), which is situated approximately 15 miles west of Old Town, to get to the city. Travelers may hire a vehicle, take a taxi or Uber from the airport to get to Split, or for 30 kuna ($5), they can take an airport shuttle that drops them off at the main bus terminal of the city.

To go by boat to the adjacent Croatian islands, go to Trajektna luka Split, which is approximately a 10-minute walk from Old Town.

Car

You may want your own vehicle if you want to go to some of the beaches and vineyards along the Dalmatian Coast in addition to Split. They are available for rental at the Split Airport as well as a number of other places throughout the city.

Remember that there are tolls on the major roads connecting, for example, Dubrovnik and Split. Additionally, rather than in miles per hour, speed restrictions are written in kilometers. Unless you want to remain for a period of time longer than three months, you won't require an international driving license.

Bus

Promet Split is the name of the local bus system, and as there isn't an English version of the website, it may be somewhat difficult for English-speaking tourists to navigate. Nevertheless, it's a cheap mode of transportation. For instance, a one-way ticket to a place in Split only costs

11 kuna (less than $2), while it only 21 kuna (less than $3.50) to go to the historic town of Trogir.

The number of zones you traverse affects fare pricing. Tickets may be purchased in advance on the bus or, at a modest discount, at a newsstand or Promet kiosk.

On Foot: The majority of Old Town is pedestrian-friendly, making foot travel the fastest method to get around the touristy districts. The car-free Marmontova Street, Riva, and Diocletian's Palace are also excellent locations to promenade.

Ferry from the port that is close to Old Town, visitors may board a ferry to go to adjacent islands including Hvar, Brac, and Vis. The cost of ferry tickets, which you may buy at the port, varies depending on how far you go. For instance, it will cost 47 kuna (about $7.50) and take around two hours to get from Split to Stari Grad, Hvar. Remember that during peak season, there will be more ferry routes available.

Taxis are an additional choice, and for the majority of local trips, they shouldn't cost more than 60 kuna (about

$10). Even yet, walking is probably the fastest option if you need to go from one end of Old Town to the other. Uber is a ride-sharing company that also has operations in Split.

COST OF A TRIP TO SPLIT

Depending on your travel preferences and budget, a trip to Split, Croatia, may cost different amounts. But the breakdown of some typical expenses you might anticipate is as follows:

From inexpensive hostels to upscale hotels, the price of lodging in Split varies substantially. You should anticipate paying between €20 and €30 per night for a dorm bed at a cheap hostel.

You should budget between €50 and €100 per night for a midrange hotel. And you should budget more than €200 per night for a nice hotel.

Food: Dining out in Split might be pricey, particularly if you go to tourist-focused establishments. However, there are also many reasonably priced eateries that provide regional food.

You may anticipate spending between €10 and €15 per person for an inexpensive supper. You should budget between €20 and €30 per person for an average lunch. And you should budget at least €50 per person for a gourmet supper.

Transportation: Traveling about Split is rather inexpensive. The city is accessible on foot, on bicycle, or by public transit. The bus fare for one person is €1.20. And a cab journey inside the city's core will run you from €5 to €10.

Activities: Split offers a wide variety of inexpensive and free activities. You may stroll along the Riva shoreline, tour the Diocletian's Palace, or go to the Museum of Croatian Archaeological Monuments.

You may attend a culinary lesson, a boat excursion to the adjacent islands, or a hike in the highlands for further unusual experiences.

Here is an example spending plan for a solitary traveler's seven-day vacation to Split:

$500 for lodging; $200 for food; and €50 for transportation.
$100 for activities
Additional costs: €50

Total: €900

MONEY-SAVING TIPS FOR BUDGET TRAVELERS

Budget-friendly travel in Split is not only feasible, but also quite rewarding. You can maximize your pleasure while controlling your costs with some advance preparation and wise decisions. Here are some suggestions for Split visitors on a tight budget:

Plan a Cheap Getaway Outside of the City.

It might be costly to stay in Split, particularly during the summer. The city receives a lot of visitors during the busy season, and the less expensive hotels are often fully booked. However, you shouldn't feel compelled to spend more to stay at a posh hotel. Accommodation prices may be greatly reduced by staying outside of the city.

The little villages of Stobre and Podstrana, located a short distance east of Split, provide hotels, hostels, guesthouses, and private rentals for a fraction of the price of a well-known hotel. It also only takes 15-20 minutes to return to Split to visit the sites.

From the Airport, Take a Bus or a Catamaran.

About 15 kilometers to the north of Split's city center lies the airport. It could be tempting to get into a cab as soon as you get at the airport exit. Taxis are quick and practical, but they are also more expensive. The good news is that there are a number of additional inexpensive methods to get from the airport to your lodging.

Examine the many bus routes that go straight from the airport to Split; the trip lasts between 30 and 40 minutes. Additionally, there is a catamaran line that travels directly into Split's city center in about 20 minutes and up to 10 times daily.

Get the SplitCard

This discount card is essential for every Split visitor who is on a tight budget. The SplitCard is free as long as you stay for at least 5 nights in the summer or 2 nights in the winter and is accessible at hotel receptions and tourist information centers all across the city.

The SplitCard offers free admission to a number of local museums, including as the City Museum and Natural History Museum, as well as special savings at a number of other museums, galleries, theaters, rental car agencies, and excursions. Additionally, it entitles you to 10% discounts at a number of eateries and stores in the Split area.

Attractions that are free or inexpensive to visit include several historical monuments in Split, such as the Diocletian's Palace and the Riva promenade. Look for free walking tours that provide an understanding of the history and culture of the city.

Book Longer-Term Lodging

Plan a minimum four-night stay to extend your stay! Consider spending at least three, four, or five nights. The pricing will be more reasonable during this time.

Don't be afraid to negotiate for the best price and request lower offers if you will be staying longer. However, keep in mind that not all apartment owners like price negotiations, so don't be offended if you are given the usual price.

Budget-Friendly Travel Advice

Don't always take a direct flight to Split, Dubrovnik, or Zagreb from the airport in Split. A flight into a low-cost gateway city, such as Milan, Bratislava, Prague, or Vienna, will be more affordable. You may get more affordable flights from there to the Croatian shore.

The best value to consider when shopping for all-inclusive packages for 3–5 star hotels is a flight/hotel bundle. The UK offers some of the most practical programs. Unbeatable offers are available from certain airlines, such as Jet2Holidays, for the Split County area, which includes Split, Hvar, Makarska (Brela), Brac, and Trogir.

Packages to the islands of Brac, Hvar, Omis, Podstrana Split City, Trogir, and all-inclusive hotels in Split are available via EasyJet Holidays.

Expediting Your Meals

Always get a menu while dining out since some proprietors (in my personal experience) prefer to charge foreign visitors more than locals. Before placing an order, compare the meal's pricing in Kuna and Euro.

Only if you are pleased with the quality of the meal and the service should you give the waiter a tip.

Currency Spending Advice

Since Croatia joined the EU a few years ago, you may bring Euros with you when you visit to save money on currency exchange costs. However, keep in mind that not all landlords of apartments or eateries (particularly those off the usual path) take Euros, so you can wind up paying an extra 10% to 15%.

Don't forget to bring your credit card, too! While American Express may not be accepted everywhere, Visa and Mastercard are always accepted.

It's still a good idea to have some Croatian Kunas on hand just in case. You may use ATM cash machines to take money out of your accounts, but because the fee can be rather hefty, I advise taking out more money. You will typically pay a fixed charge plus up to 5% in withdrawal fees each time you make a withdrawal.

Split may be the second-largest city in Croatia, but don't let size deceive you. It isn't very large. Most locations allow you to save **some money by walking** there. If money is scarce, avoid using public transportation.

Bring a reusable water bottle so you may save money and lessen your dependency on single-use plastic because Split's tap water is safe to drink. A portable filter made by LifeStraw will keep your water safe and clean.

Travel in the shoulder season since Split truly slows down in the winter, or the low season. Prices also decrease. Aim to go during the shoulder season (April–May; September–October) for somewhat warmer weather and lower lodging costs. Plan your vacation according to the season if you want to keep costs down.

Cook Your Own Meals — If money is tight, consider booking an Airbnb or hotel with a kitchen. You may then shop for food and prepare your own meals. Although it won't be fancy, it will be far less expensive than dining out often.

THINGS TO BRING ON A TRIP

What to Wear for Summer?

If you're traveling in the summer, use sunscreen every time you leave the home, particularly between 11 a.m. and 5 p.m., when insolation and heat are at their peak. Long sleeves are unlikely to be required in the evening; nevertheless, a light wind/rain jacket should suffice for unexpected rain or windy evenings.

What to Wear for Spring and Autumn Seasons?

You'll need a strong waterproof jacket on wet days. Split is a windy city all year. It is quite uncommon for rain to fall here without being accompanied by wind. Because rain is nearly always accompanied by high gusts, an umbrella provides insufficient protection. To stay dry and toasty, you should also pack a waterproof jacket and appropriate waterproof shoes.

What to Wear in Winter?

Split becomes rather chilly and damp throughout the winter season. Snow is very unusual, although it does occur on occasion. Temperatures are dropping, with mornings averaging about 6 °C (42 °F), necessitating the use of a thick, waterproof jacket. Although temperatures seldom drop below zero here, the wind chill effect has a significant influence on the 'feel like' temperature.

Strong Bura and Siloko winds, along with cold temperatures, may make you feel rather terrible, therefore excellent and warm gear is needed if you want to enjoy touring throughout the town and the surrounding region during the winter months.

Packing List

Beach Bag is a bag to transport all of your beach gear. You may even use it to carry your groceries.

Swimsuit - I suggest packing two swimsuits. They are lightweight and take up little room, but having an extra one on hand is particularly useful if you get chilly coming out of the water.

Flip Flops - Lightweight and open, having bare feet in the scorching summer heat is beneficial. Get decent ones since you'll be wearing them for most of the day.

Sunglasses - Reflections of the sun from the sea surface and the white city walls might be blinding. Most of the year, the locals here wear sunglasses.

Sunscreen is a must-have item. Sunblock is sold at local pharmacies, so you can always get it after you arrive. I propose that you bring it with you since it will most likely be considerably cheaper than purchasing it locally.

Lightweight Beach Towel - In most situations, the towels supplied in your accommodation will not contain beach towels, but rather a conventional bath, shower, and hand towel. That is why you must bring your own to the beach. Microfiber ones made of specific materials that are lightweight and dry fast are the best.

Casual Clothing - A pair of T-shirts and shorts should be enough for sightseeing. You are unlikely to need anything else. Restaurants also welcome casual attire.

A hat is a must-have for everyone visiting Dubrovnik in the summer. Choose one with a broader shade.

Sandals - Strong, durable sandals are required. In the summer, comfy sandals are the greatest option for walking around museums, cathedrals, parks, and beaches.

Because you'll be doing a lot of walking, wearing comfortable walking shoes will help you get through all of the sightseeing. Hiking boots are not required since the majority of the streets and trails are paved.

Daypacks are useful for day travel and sightseeing. Keep your water bottle (important!), camera, town map, lunch, fruit, money, and anything else that comes to mind inside. Choose one with a sturdy zip to keep your belongings secure inside.

Packable Rain Jacket - It is doubtful that you will need this jacket, but it is a good idea to have it ready in your backpack just in case.

If you want to hire a vehicle or scooter, don't forget to bring your driver's license; you won't be able to rent a car or scooter without it. If you want to undertake day excursions around Split on your own, renting a vehicle or scooter for the day is a smart choice.

If you want to drive about, an **offline SatNav GPS** device such as TomTom or similar is an excellent option. It will save you time checking your smartphone's navigation applications and will keep your phone's batteries charged and ready for any critical phone calls. Furthermore, the offline capability is quite useful since there are many regions around here where cell networks are not accessible. A nice paper map is an option.

Mains Adaptor / Travel Plug - For Split and Croatia, a Euro 2-pin mains adaptor is the best option.

USB Battery Pack / Solar Power Bank - Due to Split's high level of sunshine, solar chargers are becoming more and more common. With this device, you can power any USB device without relying on a battery or a main power source. Simply place it in a sunny location while swimming or sunbathing, and the battery will be fully charged by the end of the day. You won't have to spend time at home waiting for your phone to charge with this solar charger. And it's completely free!

Smartphone Waterproof Case - in my view, this is also a must-have item if you want to spend time at the beach. These waterproof cases are not costly and provide fantastic value for money since they provide peace of mind when using your phone near the beach where everything is wet and slippery.

Other non-essentials include:

Handbook - A decent Split handbook would be useful.

Camera - Because most individuals now have smartphones, cameras are no longer necessary. However, if you like to utilize it, you can acquire an excellent one.

Insect Repellent, Insect Spray, or Stick - if you are allergic to bug or mosquito bites, include this in your luggage as well. You can also purchase it after you arrive, although it will almost certainly be more costly.

This is not the most comprehensive packing list for Split, but it is the one that first sprang to mind since it mirrors my personal packing list when I visit Split.

HEALTH AND SAFETY ADVICE FOR TRAVELERS IN SPLIT

Even when compared to other tourist towns in Europe, Split is a fairly safe location to visit. There is occasional small thievery around tourist attractions, but applying common sense should keep you out of trouble.

Transportation and taxis are typically safe and dependable in Split, however, be wary when asking taxi drivers for suggestions of clubs or pubs, since you may be overcharged at such establishments, and use public transportation with caution.

Even if Split isn't exactly renowned for pickpockets, it's always a good idea to be cautious, particularly near prominent tourist attractions and on the beaches.

Split lies in a seismically active area; however, major earthquakes are exceedingly uncommon. Aside from that, there are no natural calamities to worry about.

Muggings and kidnappings do not occur in Split. However, it is better to avoid poorly lit neighborhoods and streets lined with pubs and clubs since they are generally populated by inebriated and belligerent individuals.

Despite the fact that there have been no recent terrorist incidents in Split, travelers should stay attentive and aware of their surroundings at all times. A series of false bomb threats have been made against shopping malls and other locations throughout Croatia, causing widespread disruption, particularly to public transportation. You should stay up to speed on local happenings and heed local government guidance.

Split is a place where you might be duped, so double-check your change and never leave your credit card unattended. Be aware of anyone who attempts to distract you by giving you unwanted aid, since this might be a ruse to steal from you.

There are no dangers to women traveling alone in Split. You may unwind, but be cautious and avoid unsafe circumstances, such as being alone with strangers or walking along dark or lonely streets.

Be cautious of unexploded mines in historically war-affected regions. Avoid leaving cultivated land or defined trails if you're traveling in these locations. Seek local guidance if in doubt.

Never go on a mountain hike or rock-climbing expedition alone.

From June through September, forest fires are prevalent. Stay vigilant for updates in the news.

Take precautions in the woods. Lyme disease and tick-borne encephalitis are potential threats. From March through September, ticks are more frequent. Ticks should be checked on your body. As quickly as possible, remove any entire ticks.

The West Nile virus may appear. No vaccine exists to guard against it. Apply insect repellant. Check that your lodging is insect-proof.

In the spring, Hemorrhagic Fever with Renal Syndrome (HFRS) ('mouse fever') is a concern in woodland settings.

When trekking in the woods, use caution. Avoid coming into touch with rats and their droppings.

Some prominent tourist sites have dress rules. If you are shirtless or wearing swimwear in locations where this is prohibited, you may be fined.

So, just how safe is Split?

Split is a highly safe tourist destination.

Crime Rates are Low: The incidence of violent crimes is low here, and the only thing you need to be concerned about are pickpockets: be cautious while strolling in a crowded crowd.

Most visitors, however, remark that things are far worse in Milan than in Split.

When going out, partying, etc., use the same prudence you would in any other situation: avoid getting into intoxicated fights and avoid strip clubs at all costs.

They are managed by Croatia's underground and shady people, with bouncers willing to beat you senseless if you refuse to pay exorbitant fees for what you bought.

If you're a woman traveling alone, there's no need to be concerned: Split is relatively secure even at night, although you should avoid wandering through abandoned areas and streets or hanging out with inebriated guys or strangers.

POPULAR SCAMS TO BE AWARE OF

It's bad that many lovely places we visit have a tiny percentage that live on taking advantage of innocent visitors who come to support their local economy. Split, Croatia is no exception, and it, too, has its share of fraud. Here's how to avoid tourist con artists in Split, Croatia.

Scam Image

When a local asks you to snap their photo, this is a common fraud in Split, Croatia. They offer you their camera and request that you photograph them. When you return the camera, they purposefully drop it and accuse you of damaging it, asking that you pay them. Please refrain from photographing anybody (unless you are certain they are not locals).

Overcharging in Taxis

When Uber and its equivalents are unavailable in a certain location, we must rely on taxis. Split, Croatia is no exception. When taking a cab in Split, always request that the meter be turned on. Planning your route ahead of time can also help you estimate how long the trip will be. This way, you may ask your taxi driver how long the journey would take before entering and compare it to what Google Maps or Waze tells you on your phone.

Helpful ATM Operator

Someone approaches you at an ATM cash machine to assist you in avoiding local bank costs. Their ultimate goal is to scan your debit or credit card with the card skimmer in their pocket and then watch you input your pin information so they may empty your account later.

Another variation of this classic scam is when your card malfunctions at an ATM machine and they approach you and offer to assist you. When inputting your pin code, always cover the number pad with your other hand.

While it's best to decline assistance at an ATM, it's much better if you can travel with credit cards that don't charge foreign currency fees and cash that can be converted at a local bank in Croatia.

"Friendly" Bar Patrons

If you want to hook up while in Split, Croatia, beware of the following scam. Two pleasant females (or men) will make small conversation and convince you that there is mutual interest. They will then advise going out for a drink and will encourage you to join them at a neighboring pub (with whom they have a partnership).

After a few shots, you'll be spending 5-10 times more. They will offer to chip in a tiny amount, but if you do not pay, you will be brought to an ATM to withdraw enough cash to cover the bill by the bar bodyguards.

There are a few things you can take to prevent falling victim to this tourist scam in Split. You may start by suggesting a bar. Second, when you arrive, ask for the bar menu so you can check the rates.

Scam of Bird Poop

When someone puts a little of white paste on your shoulder while strolling through the streets of Split, your natural reaction is to glance up, assuming it was bird feces. Suddenly, a "friendly" local offer to assist with cleanup, all while cursing the birds for making such a mess. They pickpocket you as they help you clean.

Please reject any "help" from locals who rush over to aid you unless there is an emergency. Keep all of your belongings concealed, preferably money and credit cards in an inside pocket.

Scam Guessing Game

While traveling through the streets of Split, Croatia, you see a guy with three boxes and a crowd of people attempting to predict which box the ball is in. One of the group members correctly guesses the answer, and the guy offers him money as a gift.

They repeat this with another member of the group, with the same reply. The uproar draws an increasing number of visitors to witness this charitable street entertainer. The audience is then asked to estimate by an innocent bystander. While the members of the gang are focused on where the ball is, they rapidly pickpocket them for any valuables.

Cancellations at the Last Minute

Some lodgings, although legitimate in this instance, frequently cancel your bookings within a few weeks or even days before your arrival. Why? The reasons for this vary, but in general, most hotels boost their costs at the last minute compared to when you booked your reservation, leaving you with little alternative but to pay the difference in order to avoid losing your lodging.

This is rare with respectable hosts, and these methods are highly likely to have been in place for a long period. As a result, it is prudent to thoroughly examine the evaluations of such properties or to ensure that they have visible reviews in the first place. Similarly, we suggest not just reading the best reviews, but also the negative or critical remarks.

Fake Accommodation

In recent years, it has been increasingly common to read on social media about the sad experiences of visitors who discovered, upon arrival in Croatia, that their accommodation did not exist at all.

Sites like Booking.com and Airbnb provide a large number and variety of verified accommodations, but it is likely that you have been enticed by an accommodation offer on Facebook that displayed dreamy pictures of the facilities and views, and that was also rented at a reasonable price. And, as with any reputable service for renting out space, an upfront payment is required to secure your reservation.

When you get to the provided location, there is not a single structure that matches what you saw in the images. As a result, we suggest that you avoid making bookings on portals or platforms with little assurances, or, at the very least, confirm the dependability of these lodgings ahead of time.

Pickpocketing

Distracting visitors is a popular tactic for robbers in Split to prey on them. They either converse with their victim, offer them assistance, or give them a present, and while their focus is on them, someone steals their possessions.

To reduce your pickpocketing risk, use a money belt, slash-proof bag, or anti-theft backpack. Even better, bring just what you need and leave the rest at Bounce baggage storage. Always be aware of your surroundings and suspicious of those attempting to distract you.

Scams with fake Wi-Fi

When visiting Split, avoid using free Wi-Fi. In the city, there is a typical fraud in which your personal information, accounts, and passwords are taken after connecting to a bogus network. Instead, utilize your mobile data or personal internet connection instead. To prevent having your information stolen, only connect to a trustworthy network if you absolutely must use Wi-Fi.

POPULAR ATTRACTIONS IN SPLIT YOU SHOULD SEE

Diocletian's Palace

In the center of Split, Croatia, you can find the historic architectural wonder known as Diocletian's Palace. It has enormous historical and cultural value and is one of the best-preserved Roman palaces in existence. Families on vacation will love this amazing historical location. Here is a detailed explanation to assist you in planning your visit:

Diocletian's Palace is like going back in time to a place where history is alive. You will be met by the palace's imposing walls, which have endured for ages. The palace is like a hidden city, full of mysteries just waiting to be revealed.

When you enter one of the impressive gates, a world of marvels awaits you. Elegant columns that seem to reach the sky surround the center courtyard, often referred to as the Peristyle. It resembles a big outdoor living room where people formerly gathered to celebrate and observe significant occasions. As you go through this magnificent location, you can even have a little sense of royalty.

The Cathedral of Saint Domnius is among the palace's most fascinating features. Imagine a gorgeous church with elaborate carvings and lovely artwork that was once a great emperor's mausoleum. This historic structure may be explored inside and out, and you can discover how it has changed through the years.

You may find quaint boutiques, comfortable cafés, and even some street performers as you explore the palace's labyrinthine alleys. It resembles a buried treasure trove with surprises around every turn. Both children and adults will enjoy exploring these neighborhoods, picking up interesting trinkets, and maybe even sampling some regional cuisine.

Do not overlook the palace's basement! Yes, under your feet is a secret universe. Imagine going on an adventure through deep, dark tunnels that were formerly used to store anything from supplies to secrets. Kids will love picturing what life was like in these subterranean corridors since it seems like entering a real-life adventure.

As dusk falls, the castle glows magically. An wonderful environment is produced by the warm lighting, which brings the old stones to life. You may have a nice dinner while relaxing in a welcoming restaurant while taking in the history all around you. It's the ideal way to cap off an adventurous day.

As a result, seeing Diocletian's Palace is like taking a time machine through history. With tales of emperors, lost riches, and the romance of the past, it's a great event that the entire family will treasure.

Kliss Fortress

Klis Fortress is like walking into a realm of knights, monarchs, and epic wars. You'll be astounded by the fortress's dominating position atop a rocky slope as you get closer. Perched high above the surrounding area, it is like a castle right out of a fairy tale.

Excitement will begin to grow as you make your way up to the stronghold. Even if the journey may seem a little steep, each step is worthwhile. As you approach to the fortress's entryway, picture yourself following in the footsteps of ancient soldiers.

You'll be encircled by strong stone walls that have seen centuries of history as soon as you enter the stronghold. It's as if you've stepped into a time machine where the past and present coexist together. Children will enjoy finding all the hidden treasures in the castle while picturing themselves as gallant knights guarding their realm.

The spectacular vista is among Klis Fortress's most exhilarating features. Imagine yourself perched atop the castle walls, admiring the vast surroundings below. Rolling hills, cute towns, and even the Adriatic Sea can all be seen in the distance. You'll be in awe of the scenery, and it will make for some amazing family shots.

You'll find unique rooms and passageways within the fortification. Imagine exploring the former sleeping and planning quarters of troops. Kids may let their wildest fantasies run wild as they pretend to be castle watchmen or brave explorers seeking for lost riches.

The observation towers should also be explored since they provide a panoramic perspective that will make you feel as if you are on top of the globe. Imagine looking out at the breathtaking surroundings with the wind in your hair. Your family will remember it long after your trip is over.

You could even think you're on a movie set as you roam around the stronghold. Imagine the sound of centuries-old footsteps in the hallways and the wind carrying the whispers of history. You participate in the experience as tales come to life there.

The Klis Fortress is more than simply a historical landmark; it offers an opportunity to take a trip back in time and make enduring family memories.

Cathedral of Saint Domnius

In Split, Croatia's magnificent Diocletian's Palace, the Cathedral of Saint Domnius stands as a real architectural wonder and a testament to centuries of culture, religion, and history. For tourists looking for a window into the complex history and spiritual legacy of Croatia, this cathedral is a must-visit location.

Welcome to the Cathedral of Saint Domnius, a wonderful intersection of history, art, and spirituality. As you approach this spectacular cathedral, picture walking into a realm of breathtaking beauty and historic tales.

You'll be met with an amazing building that seems to reach the skies as you approach the cathedral. You will be in awe of its complex construction and elaborate detailing. Imagine being at the entryway and gazing up at the majestic façade with its elaborate carvings and the soaring bell tower.

When you enter, you'll be overcome with awe and respect for everything there. The cathedral's interior is like a museum filled with fascinating artifacts and a peaceful environment. Take a moment to picture yourself strolling on chilly stone floors that have heard the footfall of innumerable tourists throughout the years.

You can't help but be charmed by the magnificent dome that appears to reach the sky if you look up. Stained glass windows allow sunlight to seep through, creating a kaleidoscope of colors that dance over the walls and floor.

Consider taking a minute to relax in a serene location and consider the beauty and history that are all around you.

The altar is one of the cathedral's most alluring elements. Imagine a golden work of art that is lavishly decorated with complex figures and decorations. Your family will be in awe at the sight, and it will spark discussions on the skill and commitment that went into its creation.

A historic baptistery, where generations have been baptized into the religion, is also housed in the cathedral. As you go around this holy place, consider the echoes of baptisms from ages before. It serves as a reminder of the significance of the cathedral in countless individuals' lives throughout time.

The crypt, a secret cavern under the church, will fascinate children. Imagine ascending the stairs and entering a dimly lit area rich with history and artifacts. It's a location that piques interest and encourages people to let their imaginations go wild with historical tales.

Take a minute to once again take in the elaborate elements of the outside as you exit the church. Consider the artisans who devoted their talents to producing this masterpiece, leaving their imprint on history for future generations.

The Cathedral of Saint Domnius is more than simply a structure; it is a symbol of human ingenuity, religious belief, and the passage of time.

Marjan Forest Park

Croatia's Marjan Forest Park, a tranquil sanctuary perched on a peninsula overlooking Split, is a paradise for nature lovers, families, and anybody wanting a break from the bustle of the city. This Park is a lush haven where visitors may enjoy outdoor activities, peace, and stunning vistas, all of which combine to make for an amazing experience.

Croatia's Marjan Forest Park is like walking into a world of untouched nature, adventure, and leisure. With a range of attractions that will enthrall visitors of all ages, this magical park is the ideal holiday spot for families. Here is a detailed explanation to assist you in planning your visit:

On a lovely peninsula with a view of the glistening Adriatic Sea, Marjan Forest Park is a verdant haven. Cool air and the soft rustling of leaves will greet you as you get closer, creating the mood for a day of outdoor exploration.

Marjan might be thought of as a vast playground built by nature itself. Imagine yourself strolling down meandering paths among aromatic pine trees, the light glinting through the branches. The park's thick foliage acts as a living carpet that welcomes you to enter a quiet and fascinating world.

Prepare yourself for breathtaking sights that will leave you speechless. Imagine yourself at vantage positions with expansive views of the azure water, the attractive city of Split, and the far-off islands. It's like being in the center of nature's masterpiece, with a vista that will live on in your mind forever.

Family-Friendly Attractions: Marjan Forest Park is a family-friendly haven. Imagine going on a walk as a family where the kids may look for secret paths and learn about the forest's mysteries. All ages and physical levels may join in and enjoy the trip thanks to the park's paths.

Outdoor Adventures: For those looking for a little more thrill, consider rock climbing the challenging cliffs with knowledgeable experts. Parents and children may both take on new challenges, face their anxieties, and celebrate victories together.

Relaxation & Picnics: Picture selecting the ideal location for a family outing while surrounded by the calming rustle of leaves and the pleasant aroma of pine trees. Spread a blanket out, prepare your favorite foods, and spend quality time together as a family in the middle of nature.

Historical Finds: As you go around the park, you can come upon historic landmarks and old hermitages. Imagine discovering these peaceful nooks and learning the tales of the past. It offers young people a concrete and interesting method to relate to history.

Beaches and Playgrounds: Marjan Forest Park also has isolated beaches where children may play unrestrictedly, create sandcastles, and paddle in the glistening seas. Imagine hearing the sound of children laughing as they plunge into the ocean, their faces beaming with joy.

Moments of Serenity: If you're a parent looking for a moment of calm, try finding a quiet place to sit and relax while you read a book or take in the scenery. In the middle of your family journey, it's an opportunity to relax and rediscover your equilibrium.

You're not simply on vacation when you visit Marjan Forest Park; you're also starting a journey into the embrace of nature. It's a setting for creating memories, building relationships, and seeing the marvels of the globe.

Riva Promenade

Welcome to the Riva Promenade, the beating heart and spirit of Split, Croatia. Imagine a stunning cityscape with a shoreline where the Adriatic's allure meets the city's vibrant pulse. The Riva Promenade is a bustling meeting spot that combines history, culture, and the peaceful lapping of the sea.

The calm sound of soft waves and the energizing smell of the sea wind will welcome you as you get closer. It's a location where excitement and leisure coexist together.

Playful Exploration: Picture yourself strolling hand in hand with your children down a broad promenade that hugs the glistening sea. Palm palms that border The Riva offer shaded areas ideal for a brief rest or a family selfie. Parents may enjoy the peace of mind that comes with a car-free area while letting their children run about freely.

Cafés on the Waterfront: The Riva is a fun area for people of all ages. Think of relaxing in a welcoming café that overlooks the water. The kids may have exquisite ice cream as the parents enjoy their favorite beverages. The cafés are lively venues where your family may experience the local culture in addition to being places to dine and drink.

Stunning Sunsets: As the day draws to a close, the Riva transforms into a wonderful location to see the sunset. Visualize an orange, pink, and gold-hued sky that illuminates the water with a cozy warmth. Sitting on the edge of the promenade, the whole family can marvel as the sun disappears below the horizon.

Lively Events: During festivals and events, the Riva Promenade is a hive of activity. Imagine stumbling onto a live music performance, a street show, or an arts and crafts fair. While parents take in the vibrant ambiance, children might be enthralled by the music and colors.

Sea Adventures: If your family enjoys the ocean, consider leaving from the Riva on a boat cruise. Consider sailing the Adriatic, going on an adventure to a secret grotto, and possibly even seeing dolphins playing in the surf. It's an opportunity to have cherished family experiences on the wide seas.

Historic structures that convey tales about the city's history may be seen as you stroll around the Riva. Imagine pausing to appreciate the building's design and maybe learning a little about the region's past. It's similar to fitting some learning into a family vacation.

Views: The Riva Promenade provides some of the outstanding panoramas of Split's historic district and its surroundings. Think of the tales those wonderful red-roofed structures could carry as you gaze across the water at them. It is a picture-perfect representation of Croatia's shoreline.

Zlatni Rat Beach

Welcome to Zlatni Rat Beach, a natural wonder that adorns the Croatian coast. Think of a beach where the form and color appear to vary with the tides, where the Adriatic Sea meets the land in a breathtaking display of beauty and tranquility.

Golden Beauty: Zlatni Rat Beach, often known as the "Golden Horn" or the "Golden Cape," is like a painting that nature herself has drawn. Imagine a thin, sandy tongue jutting out into the Adriatic's azure seas. The golden sand of the beach glows in the warmth of the sun, creating a surreal atmosphere.

Zlatni Rat Beach is distinguished for its distinctive shape. Imagine a tip that is constantly bending and moving in response to the wind and currents. The beach seems to have a life of its own and responds to the whims of the elements. Your family will have access to a variety of viewpoints and a feeling of adventure thanks to its unusual design.

Crystal Clear Waters: Visualize yourself swimming in the Adriatic Sea's crystal-clear waters. Here, the sea is more than simply a swimming hole; it's a playground of blue colours that begs you to lose yourself in its cooling embrace. Imagine exploring the vibrant marine life that resides in these waters while snorkeling with your children.

Water Sports and Adventure: Zlatni Rat Beach provides a range of water activities for families looking for a little more adventure. Just picture yourself paddling, paddleboarding, or windsurfing with your loved ones. It's a chance for people to connect over a common passion and make lifelong memories.

The open, sun-drenched length is alluring, but Zlatni Rat Beach also has areas that are sheltered by scented pine trees. Imagine securing a comfortable location among the trees, letting the kids play in the sand while you unwind in the refreshing shade. It strikes a balance between sun and shade that meets the requirements of the whole family.

Stunning Views: Zlatni Rat Beach offers an absolutely stunning outlook. Think of relaxing on the beach and admiring the Adriatic Sea's boundless horizon. You'll feel as if you're in a picture-postcard setting as you take in the sight of sailboats skimming over the sea and far-off islands in the distance.

Local Flavor: There are pubs and cafés on each side of the beach where you may relax and eat food from your region. Imagine relishing delicious seafood dishes, drinking cool beverages, and enjoying Croatian tastes. It's an opportunity to enjoy the local food and culture next to the ocean.

Split Archaeological Museum

Welcome to the Split Archaeological Museum, a site where historical relics, archeological finds, and a rich tapestry of cultures bring history to life. Imagine entering a world of discovery where you and your family may solve historical puzzles and learn more about the ancient civilizations that previously inhabited this area.

The Split Archaeological Museum is like a treasure trove of historical artifacts. Imagine strolling through rooms filled with relics from ancient times, each of which has an own tale to tell. The museum is a tribute to the artistry and creativity of ancient peoples, with beautiful ceramics, delicate jewelry, colossal sculptures, and elaborate mosaics.

For families, the museum is an educational excursion that doubles as a center of learning. Imagine the excitement in your children's eyes as they see realistic representations of ancient life, ancient weaponry, and ancient equipment. It's an opportunity for parents to encourage inquiry and pique their kids' historical interest.

Treasures from the Past: Picture yourself in front of a Roman gravestone, imagining the lives of people who lived hundreds of years ago. Roman antiquities, Greek pottery, and even Egyptian items may be found in the museum's collection. It is a voyage through several cultures and civilizations, giving insight into the varied past of the area.

The museum includes interactive displays to further enhance the interest in history. Think of seeing archeological sites online or learning how to understand old writing. These exhibitions encourage you and your family to actively engage in the educational process.

Local Context: The Split Archaeological Museum serves as a link between the history and present of the area in addition to being a storehouse for artifacts. Imagine being able to explain how ancient civilizations impacted Split and its surroundings, influencing the region's identity to this day.

The museum also has magnificent specimens of prehistoric art. Imagine being in front of magnificent frescoes and gorgeous sculptures that have withstood the test of time.

Ancient civilizations' creative creations are brought to life, inspiring admiration for genius that knows no boundaries.

Croatian National Theatre

The majestic Croatian National Theatre, a cultural gem that displays the city's creative past and provides access to a wide range of enthralling performances, is located right in the center of Split, Croatia. Imagine a location where history, creativity, and the arts all come together to invite you to experience the wonder of theater, opera, ballet, and music.

Architectural Masterpiece: The Croatian National Theatre in Split is a striking example of architectural elegance. Imagine yourself in front of its imposing façade, which is embellished with elaborate sculptures, lavish decorations, and imposing columns. The architecture of the building conveys a feeling of timeless beauty, which is a reflection of the city's significant historical and cultural past.

Cultural Heartbeat: Entering the theater will immerse you in a world where the arts are alive. Imagine the excitement in the air as you walk into the auditorium, surrounded by magnificent furnishings. The theater acts as the beating heart of the culture, throbbing with the vitality of the performances that take place there.

Excellence in Theatre: Visualize taking your seat, the lights fading, and the curtain opening to show an engrossing performance. The Croatian National Theatre presents a wide range of theatrical productions, including both classic and modern works. The theater immerses you in the world of the characters and their story with each word said and each emotion conveyed.

Operatic Grandeur: The Croatian National Theatre provides opera fans with a magical experience. Imagine being mesmerized by opera singers' rousing voices as they fly across the theater with passion and elegance. The stage comes to life with lavish costumes and gripping storytelling that transports you to the ageless realm of opera.

Brilliant Ballet: Ballet fans will be mesmerized by the elegance and beauty of the ballet performances the theater presents. Imagine seeing dancers perform with grace and accuracy while narrating tales with their movements. Ballet artists create works of art that use movement to evoke strong emotions on a canvas that is the theater.

Symphonic Harmony: The theater's symphonic performances will appeal to music lovers. Visualize the symphony orchestra entering the room, each note resonating with brilliant melodies. Because of the hall's acoustics, you can really feel the music, which creates an emotional experience.

Cultural Heritage: The Croatian National Theatre serves as a custodian of Croatia's cultural heritage and is more than just a performance space. Imagine being a part of a custom that stretches back to the late 19th century, where the theater preserves and honors the culture of the country. Croatia's dedication to fostering and protecting its cultural identity is reflected in the theater.

People's Square (Pjaca)

Discover the lovely People's Square, also known as Pjaca, in the heart of Split's old district. Imagine a busy square that is a vibrant center of history, culture, and community as well as a physical location. People's Square has a lively and alluring ambiance as a result of the confluence of centuries' worth of life, tales, and customs.

People's Square is comparable to a crossroads in time, where history is brought to life by the buildings, cobblestone streets, and the energy of the people who have congregated here for decades. Imagine traveling in the footsteps of the Romans of antiquity, the merchants of the Middle Ages, and the residents of today, who have all left their stamp on this historic area.

Charming Architecture: As you approach People's Square, you'll see a fusion of architectural motifs that pay homage to the city's rich history. Visualize gazing up at the façade of buildings with ornate embellishments, Venetian-style arches, and vibrant shutters that provide the area a welcoming feel.

Cafés & Gathering Places: Adorable cafés and restaurants with outdoor seating edge the plaza, providing a warm atmosphere. Picture yourself relaxing at a café table, drinking a cup of Croatian coffee or eating a meal while taking in the sights. More than simply places to dine, these cafés serve as gathering spots for residents and visitors to swap tales and make memories.

Imagine a gorgeous stone fountain with figures that seem to be dancing with delight in the heart of People's Square. This ancient fountain is more than simply a pretty feature; it's a place where people congregate and has been the scene of innumerable discussions, giggles, and moments of relaxation.

Local Markets & Events: People's Square is a vibrant location where these things take place. Imagine yourself perusing kiosks stocked with handmade items, fresh food, and regional crafts. The area transforms into a bustling market where you can interact with local merchants and learn about the cuisine and crafts of Croatia.

Historic Landmarks: There are important landmarks close to People's Square that enrich the experience. Consider touring the city's historical Venetian clock tower, which dates back to the fifteenth century. The tower's chimes signal the passage of time and contribute to the charming ambiance of the area.

Cultural Connection: The square is more than simply a tourist attraction; it serves as a hub for community activities, festivals, and cultural celebrations. Think about finding a traditional dance, an art show, or a live performance. People's Square serves as a platform for the cultural manifestations of the city.

SOME OFF-THE-BEATEN-PATH DESTINATIONS IN SPLIT

Finding secret jewels, lesser-known locations, and one-of-a-kind experiences in Split may be accomplished by traveling to off-the-beaten-path locations. The following locations guarantee to show this Croatian city in a unique light:

The picturesque area of **Veli Varo** is a labyrinth of winding lanes, stone homes, and little squares. Explore its lanes, take in the neighborhood vibe, and find charming cafés and genuine restaurants.

Diocletian's Palace is a popular tourist destination, yet many people overlook **Jupiter's Temple Crypt**, which is located under the Peristyle. Investigate this undiscovered cavern that once served as a pagan temple.

Fruit's Square (Voni trg) is a charming place to grab a coffee or ice cream that is situated away from the major roads. It's a local favorite since it provides a tranquil atmosphere away from the masses.

Marjan Forest Park is well-known, but **Marjan Hill** Lookout Points also provide breathtaking views of Split and the Adriatic Sea. For panoramic vistas, think about going to Telegrin and Vidilica.

Froggyland: This odd museum has more than 500 stuffed frogs doing human-like tasks. It's a peculiar yet captivating experience that often astounds guests.

Gripe Fort: Although the stronghold isn't often at the top of tourists' agendas, it offers a peaceful haven from the bustle of the city and gives an alternative viewpoint of Split.

The remote beach of **Kamen Brela** is just a short drive from Split but is less popular with visitors since it is concealed behind a tiny hill. The trip is worthwhile due to its unspoiled beauty.

Even though **St. Michael's Fortress** is not in Split, a day trip to Ibenik to visit it is a worthwhile off-the-beaten-path adventure. The castle provides stunning vistas and historical insights.

You may learn about the fascinating history of the **Alka Knight's** game and its relevance to the area at the Sinjska Alka Museum, which is located close by in the town of Sinj. The museum provides insight into a distinctive cultural practice.

Bavice Cemetery: This ancient graveyard is situated on Marjan Hill and provides a calm atmosphere for reflection. Additionally, it's a secret location to take in expansive city views.

Explore the less well-known ancient city of **Salona** near Split at the Solin Archaeological Museum. The extensive history of the area is shown by the archaeological museum.

Again, not in Split but yet readily reached, the **Medvedgrad Fortress** near Zagreb has magnificent medieval architecture, picturesque scenery, and historical importance.

Kastel Gomilica: Gomilica, one of the seven Kastela settlements, is a charming beach community halfway between Split and Trogir.

NEARBY DAY TRIPS FROM SPLIT

There are several enjoyable day excursion possibilities from Split that are close by for a holiday. You may enjoy the following amazing day excursions from Split:

About a 1.5-hour drive from Split lies **Krka National Park,** which is renowned for its entrancing waterfalls and glistening blue-green waters. Families may take leisurely strolls along wooden paths that pass by gushing waterfalls and verdant woodlands. Bring your swimwear, since swimming is permitted in a few authorized sites.

Despite being a little farther away (approximately a 2.5 to 3-hour drive), **Plitvice Lakes National Park** is well worth the trip. The beautiful environment of this UNESCO World Heritage Site is made up of a network of interconnecting lakes and waterfalls. Families may enjoy a boat trip on the serene lakes and explore the park on well-maintained pathways.

Trogir: Trogir, a gorgeous medieval town with winding alleyways, historic structures, and attractive squares, is just 30 minutes from Split by car. You may visit historical monuments like the Kamerlengo Fortress and the Trogir Cathedral on a leisurely walk across the area.

Omis: Located at the mouth of the Cetina River, Omis is just about a 40-minute drive from Split and provides both scenic natural beauty and outdoor recreation. Families may hike, zip line, and go river rafting in the breathtaking Cetina River canyon.

Hvar Island: To enjoy the energetic environment of this well-liked resort, take the boat from Split to Hvar Island (it takes about 1.5 hours). Beautiful buildings, a former fortress, and picturesque cobblestone streets are all features of Hvar Town. Families may relax on the beaches and take part in aquatic activities.

The island of **Brac**, famous for its popular Zlatni Rat beach, is just a short boat journey from Split. Families may enjoy a day of swimming, tanning, and water sports. Explore the local cuisine, shopping, and culture in the town of Bol on Bra.

Salona Archaeological Park: The remains of the old Roman city of Salona are just a 15-minute drive from Split and provide an interesting look into the past. The ruins of temples, amphitheaters, and other buildings may be explored by families as a historical and educational excursion.

In addition to the things to do in Omis, you can also take in the breathtaking natural beauty of the **Cetina River and the canyon** that surrounds it. Families may go kayaking or on guided boat cruises to enjoy the tranquility of the river.

Blue Lagoon: A paradise for swimming and snorkeling, the Blue Lagoon is accessible by boat from Split. It's a great place for a calm family day excursion because of the pristine seas, abundant marine life, and tranquil setting.

The medieval fortress of **Klis** is only a short drive from Split and provides sweeping views of the region. Given that it was featured in the well-known television series "*Game* of *Thrones*," it is particularly fascinating for families with older children.

Mostar

Even if you don't have any more explorations of Croatia's neighbor, Bosnia-Herzegovina, planned, we strongly advise taking a day excursion from Split to explore Mostar's old town.

A day trip is sufficient to see the main attractions of this stunning city center.

The most recognizable landmark in Mostar's Old Town is unquestionably Stari Most, a stunning bridge that spans the Neretva River.

Visitors who come throughout the day may witness divers plunge from the bridge into the frigid river below in exchange for money.

Go to the middle of Lucky Most, the famous bridge across the river, for a fantastic view of Stari Most. From the banks of the Neretva River, you may also take pictures of the bridge.

For stunning views of the Old Town, climb the Koski Mehmed Pasha Mosque's tower.

For souvenir shopping, stroll the cobblestoned alleys and explore the bazaars.

If you wish to understand more about Mostar's past and the 1990s Balkans War, which resulted in Stari Most's destruction, take a historical walking tour.

OUTDOOR ACTIVITIES IN SPLIT

Split is quickly emerging as the go-to location for outdoor adventure in not just Croatia but also all of central Europe, and it also has the UNESCO-listed Palace of Diocletian. Here are some of Split's best outdoor activities.

Cycling Tour

On this 3-hour bike trip, see the main Split attractions as well as local favorites like Marjan Hill, the city's lungs.

Ride a normal bike or an electric bike through aromatic pine trees, picturesque lookouts, and historic churches in this mountainous nature reserve.

Hiking

The four-hour hike begins in the city's core. This leisurely walking trip is designed to accommodate all levels of fitness along the paths that wind through Marjan Hill's lush woodland.

Marjan (178m) is the ideal location for anybody looking to escape the bustle of the city while yet enjoying stunning views of Split and the adjacent islands (Solta, Hvar, Brac).

Rock Climb

Get transportation from Split for a 4-hour rock climbing trip to Marjan Hill's ragged limestone cliffs! The experience includes the use of all climbing tools, including ropes, harnesses, and a belay, and is guided by a local climbing instructor. Discover methods like top-rope climbing, then try them out for yourself!

All skill levels, from novice to expert, may enjoy excellent climbing conditions in the area around Marjan Hill.

Tour by Kayak

The best outdoor activities in Split during the summer include a 4-hour sea-kayaking excursion around the Marjan peninsula, paddling across the water to Ciovo island, and exploring quiet coves and pristine beaches.

It is possible to expand this journey to a 6 or 8-hour tour of adjacent islands if you have extra time on your hands. Both excursions include a safety lecture and a life jacket, and they both begin and end in Split. No specialized knowledge is needed.

Tour of the Seas

Set off from Split on a boat to cruise the magnificent island of Ciovo, stopping along the way to go swimming or snorkeling at some of its beautifully remote beaches.

Act as a member of the crew and assist with ship management throughout the 4-hour sailing excursion under the watchful eye of a knowledgeable guide.

Just a willingness to actively engage while taking in the views of Croatia's stunning island environment will do; no previous expertise is necessary. Upgrade to a full-day trip if you have more time available, and have a light lunch at one of the island's eateries.

Food & Wine Tasting with Diverse Activities

The ideal way to begin your evening activities is with a 3-hour evening walking tour of Split and wine sampling.

The itinerary comprises a leisurely walk along the main avenue (Riva), a visit to Marjan Hill and the historic Varos neighborhood, and a wine sampling.

It's an excellent chance to ask the bar's sommelier about the history of Croatian wine and obtain advice on which wine is best to take home.

Rafting

Rafting on the Cetina River is a distinct draw for all adventure seekers and is perhaps the most well-known adventure excursion in the region.

One of the most picturesque rivers in Croatia is the Cetina, which has caves, waterfalls, rapids, and peaceful sections. Through pristine scenery and water that is crystal-clear, it combines adventure and relaxation.

You may have a BBQ meal on the riverbanks when the rafting is over. Everyone who has the guts to participate in this unique event will never forget it and probably return for more.

Cetina River serves as the setting for the exciting activity of **canyoning**. Beautiful rocky landscapes with cliffs up to 180 meters high may be seen at Cetina Canyon. Be prepared to be astounded by the natural landscape you will encounter, which is beyond your wildest dreams.

You will traverse rivers and rapids, swim in natural pools, travel through underground tunnels, and go around lakes and waterfalls, including the 55-meter-high Gubavica waterfall, while canyoning. If you're searching for the whole adventure package, this encounter is one of a kind. Remember that safety comes first, and respect the force of nature.

Zipline

The zipline experience is quite unique, particularly when it is carried out in the forest next to a river. Eight steel lines totaling 2.1 kilometers in length are used for ziplining to span the canyon. The longest wire is located at a height of 150 meters and is 700 meters long. It is absolutely safe, and all of the tour leaders are licensed and experienced.

You should take advantage of this chance to go beyond your comfort zone and have fun. Your heart will start to beat a bit quicker as you engage in this adrenaline-pumping exercise, but you'll also wonder why you waited so long to give it a try.

Skydiving

The flush of adrenaline has not yet subsided. What do you think about going into free fall? Together with a trained skydiving instructor, you will jump out of an aircraft, and they will make sure everything goes according to plan so you may relax and enjoy to the utmost.

Skydiving is a life-altering activity, and you will probably always remember the instant when you jumped out of the aircraft. Numerous participants report that it was both incredibly motivating and a little addicting. Your priorities in life will definitely alter after 60 seconds of free fall!

Horse Riding

In Split, horseback riding is another option for an active vacation. A few organizations provide beginning riding clinics or provide horseback riding for fun. The most common pastime is field horseback riding, which is a great joy for all riders.

Exploring the countryside and getting in touch with nature may both be done while riding. Many of the trips conclude with meal breaks and opportunities to connect with friendly locals.

Paintball

Time to play some paintball! There are several reasons for this, including the fact that it is an excellent way to socialize and spend time with friends or make new ones.

It's enjoyable, it's played outside, and it brings out your inner kid, particularly in terms of competitiveness. Even though it's a war game, it pulls people closer since they stick together as they battle! Do you really need an excuse to give it a shot?

Outdoor Yoga and Fitness Sessions: Split's beautiful splendor is used in many outdoor yoga and fitness sessions. You can work out while unwinding and breathing fresh air thanks to outdoor fitness boot camps and yoga sessions by the water.

Make sure you have the right gear, adhere to safety precautions, and take the weather into account before engaging in any outside activity. The organization of your outdoor experiences in and around Split is made simple by the availability of several activities via regional tour operators.

A PERFECT SEVEN-DAY ITINERARY FOR A VISIT TO SPLIT

Here's a comprehensive 7-day itinerary for an enjoyable visit to Split, Croatia. This itinerary includes a mix of historical exploration, outdoor activities, cultural experiences, and relaxation:

Day 1: Arrival and Old Town Exploration

Arrive in Split and check in to your accommodation.

Start your trip with a walk-through Diocletian's Palace, a UNESCO World Heritage Site. Explore the Peristyle, the Cathedral of Saint Domnius, and the underground cellars.

Enjoy a leisurely dinner at a local restaurant within the palace walls.

Day 2: Marjan Hill and Seafront

Begin your day with a hike or bike ride up Marjan Hill. Take in panoramic views of Split and the Adriatic Sea.

After descending, have lunch at a seaside restaurant on Riva Promenade.

Spend your afternoon relaxing at Bačvice Beach, swimming, sunbathing, or playing picigin, a traditional beach game.

Evening strolls along Riva Promenade and enjoy street performances.

Day 3: Island Hopping - Hvar

Take an early morning ferry to Hvar Island.

Explore Hvar Town's charming streets, visit the historic fortress, and enjoy lunch at a local restaurant.

Relax on one of the island's beautiful beaches or participate in water activities.
Return to Split in the evening and have dinner at a local konoba (tavern).

Day 4: Trogir and Ciovo Island

Take a day trip to Trogir, a UNESCO-listed town. Explore its historic center, visit St. Lawrence Cathedral, and stroll along the waterfront.

In the afternoon, take a short boat ride to Ciovo Island for some beach time and snorkeling.

Return to Split and enjoy a seafood dinner at a restaurant near the sea.

Day 5: Krka National Park

Join a guided day trip to Krka National Park. Enjoy the stunning waterfalls, walk along the wooden pathways, and have a picnic lunch.

If time allows, stop in the charming town of Šibenik on your way back to Split.

Have a relaxing evening by taking a sunset walk along Marjan Hill's scenic trails.

Day 6: Outdoor Adventures - Zip-Lining and Rafting

Take a day trip to Omiš for outdoor adventures.
Start with a thrilling zip-lining experience over the Cetina River canyon.

After zip-lining, enjoy a local lunch in Omiš.

In the afternoon, go white-water rafting on the Cetina River for an adrenaline-pumping adventure.

Return to Split in the evening and have a farewell dinner at a restaurant with a sea view.

Day 7: Relaxation and Departure

Spend your last morning in Split at a local café, enjoying a leisurely breakfast.

If you haven't had a chance to visit any museums, explore the Split City Museum or the Archaeological Museum.

Take some time for last-minute souvenir shopping.

Depending on your departure time, enjoy your final moments in Split, and depart for the airport or your next destination.

Remember that this itinerary is just a suggestion, and you can adjust it based on your interests and preferences. Additionally, make sure to check the opening hours and availability of attractions, activities, and tours in advance to ensure a smooth and enjoyable trip.

CULTURAL FESTIVALS AND HOLIDAYS

You may participate in the following cultural events and festivals in Split:

Split Summer Festival (Splitsko ljeto): Usually held from mid-July to mid-August, this is one of Croatia's most renowned and earliest cultural events. A wide range of theater, music, dance, and visual arts acts are presented throughout the festival. Cultural events that honor both domestic and foreign artists animate the historical areas of Diocletian's Palace and other locations across the city.

Days of Diocletian (Dani Dioklecijana): This event, which is held every year in late August, is a historical recreation of Roman life in honor of Emperor Diocletian, who constructed the palace in the 4th century. The celebration features a variety of events, including gladiator battles, Roman parades, and traditional artisan exhibitions. Within the royal walls, visitors may see the history of the city come to life.

Split Film Festival: This global event features cutting-edge and independent movies from all around the globe. It takes place in September and provides a platform for up-and-coming filmmakers as well as a fantastic chance for movie fans to see a wide variety of cinematic works.

Ethnoambient Solin Festival: This festival honors traditional and international music, dance, and art and is held in the adjacent town of Solin. Folk groups, ethnomusical bands, and performers from various ethnic origins often perform as part of it. It's an exceptional chance to discover the variety of global cultures via music and dance.

Dani Marulia's "Days of Maruli": This event, which honors the Croatian Renaissance poet Marko Maruli, generally takes place in April. Readings, poetry recitals, exhibits, and debates on literature, philosophy, and culture are all included in this literary and cultural event.

Mediterranean Film Festival Split: This yearly occasion focuses on movies that investigate the socioeconomic problems, culture, and way of life in the Mediterranean region. It serves as a forum for filmmakers to discuss experiences and viewpoints from this area, promoting cross-cultural communication.

Split Wine and Gastronomy Event: This event is a pleasure for wine and cuisine lovers. It usually takes place in November and features regional wines, heirloom foods, and cooking demonstrations. It's an opportunity to experience Dalmatia's delicacies and discover its culinary history.

Gallery and Museum Exhibits: Throughout the year, Split's galleries and museums offer a variety of exhibits that highlight local artists, historical objects, and works of modern and traditional art. Among the attractions to visit are the Metrovi Gallery, Split City Museum, and Ivan Metrovi Studio.

Traditional Folk Performances: Look for folk dance and music shows that honor the regional tradition and culture. Public squares, urban parks, and cultural settings are often the locations of these gatherings.

Artisan Workshops: A few regional craftsmen provide classes where guests may learn how to make ceramics, weave, and paint. These events provide participants with a practical understanding of Dalmatian culture.

To find out about forthcoming celebrations and cultural events that will take place during your vacation dates, consult regional event calendars and tourist websites while organizing your trip to Split. Participating in these activities will enhance your knowledge of the city's cultural legacy and provide you with life-changing experiences while you're there.

BEST BEACHES IN SPLIT

Jezinac Beach

Jezinac Beach is situated in the heart of Split, about one kilometer from the city's core. With a brilliant, fine-pebble beach, fantastic palm palms, spectacular turquoise water hues, and the little castle Mestrovic Kastilac in the distance, this amazing bay captures the imagination.

While snorkeling in this area of the shore, the water is exceptionally clear and you can observe a lot of fish. The beach amenities are excellent as well! The Jezinac beach has restrooms with showers, changing areas, and parking.

A café also provides snacks and a stunning view of the ocean. One of the nicest beaches in Split is unquestionably Jezinac Beach, which is also close to the old town.

Kasjuni Beach

Many people believe Kasjuni Beach, which is situated on the southern edge of Marjan Forest Park, to be Split's most beautiful beach. This long, gorgeous bay excels because of its idyllic pebble beach, clean water, and welcoming holiday vibe.

Another breathtaking view is of the cliffs at Marjan Forest Park. The trendy Beach Club in Plaza Kasjuni, which is situated at the upper end of the cove, is also well-known. The guideline is to "observe and be observed."

At the chic Joes Beach Bar, you may get a refreshing drink and take in the stunning ocean view if you'd like, or you can rent sun loungers and umbrellas. The beach becomes more laid-back and even has a spot for dogs as you go farther south.

Sand Beach Bacvice

The most well-known sandy beach in Split and one of the most well-liked bathing beaches in the heart of the city is the Plaza Bacvice. It is perfect for non-swimmers and elderly persons as well as families with young children due to how shallow it is.

The port and ferry are easily accessible due to its close proximity to the city center, and the old town is just a 10-minute walk away. In this 600-meter-long bay, there is constant activity. There are several beach bars, snack shops, and restaurants to keep you occupied, and umbrellas and sun loungers may be hired at an affordable fee.

This beach is suggested in the low season when things are a little more laid back for those looking for peace and quiet.

Ovcice Beach

The Ovcice Beach is a great recommendation for enjoying some fantastic beach days in Split is Ovcice. This coastal strip, which is quite close to the city center and is just around the corner from the Bacvice beach, is made up of numerous lovely tiny coves.

This location is unquestionably one of the nicest beaches in Split and is well-liked by both young and elderly people. The water is very clean and brilliantly blue in this location. Additionally, although being far more tranquil than the bustling nearby beach, this cove still offers a decent range of beach bars, as well as showers and changing areas.

If you arrive by vehicle, there is a parking area just adjacent to the beach. An excellent beach that is conveniently located near Split's old town.

Znjan Beach

The Znjan Beach is Split's stunning, recently constructed city beach, making it a genuine insider travel recommendation. This magnificent pebble beach includes several little coves with exquisite water hues and a distinctive vacation ambiance for swimming and bathing.

Particularly on weekends, there are several pubs and restaurants that provide entertainment. Families with kids will enjoy themselves here as well! There are trampolines, playgrounds, bounce houses, and different thrilling water activities. One of Split's most well-liked beaches,

Znjan Beach is where residents and visitors come together to enjoy amazing summer days on the Adriatic.

Trstenik Beach

On Split's generally bustling shore, the Tristenik Beach stands out as a very lovely beach. It is also one of the bays with the least amount of activity. Visitors like the laid-back ambiance they may experience here while on vacation.

This coastal area excels in many ways. Here, the gravel is virtually sandy and provides a straightforward entrance to the ocean. Additionally, the water is very clean and ideal for snorkeling.

Everyone can find a comfortable spot to enjoy the Croatian sun thanks to the long bay's ample area as well. Families with kids, couples, and people looking for solitude all like visiting this bay. One of Split's nicest beaches is located away from the crowds.

Radisson Beach

The bay of the Radisson Blu Hotel is one of the nicest beaches in Split and comes highly recommended. In actuality, the hotel consistently maintains this beautiful area of Plaza Trestenik. As a result, the whole beach is spotless and great for swimming.

Of course, non-hotel visitors are also welcome to lay out their towels and swim in the clear water. You may pamper yourself to a VIP sun lounger if you'd like, or you can have a drink at one of Split's hippest beach clubs, Mistral Bar & Restaurant.

This section of shoreline is perfect for kiteboarding and surfing when the wind is blowing, so water sports aficionados will also like it.

Firule Beach

One of Split's most exquisite sandy beaches, Firule Beach is about 1.5 kilometers from the city center. The lovely bay is bordered by trees that offer shade, particularly during the sweltering summer, and give the coastline a lovely Mediterranean feel.

Additionally, the fine sand beach has a relatively modest slope, making it one of the city's most well-liked swimming areas, especially for families with young children.

The amenities are even another perk! For instance, Firule Beach has a café with a stunning view of the bay, a bakery close by, plus showers and changing facilities. Additionally, a few parking spots are located just above the water.

Stobrec Jug Beach

In the vicinity of Split, the Stobrec Jug Beach promises to be a superb swimming highlight. This stunning bay is part of the well-known resort Stobrec and is approximately 9 kilometers from Split's city center.

You'll get complete bathing enjoyment while on vacation there. Swimming is encouraged in the crystal-clear sea, which has the most exquisite sea hues, and the fine pebble beach makes it simple to enter the refreshing water. Additionally, the pebbles are really white, which makes a stunning contrast to the blue water and green pine trees.

The café above the bay, which is a well-kept secret, has a magnificent view of the coastline. An unquestionably fantastic beach for a holiday in the Split region.

Bene Beach

One of Split's oldest beaches, lovely Bene Beach lies tucked away in the Marjan forest park. It is picturesquely tucked up amongst tall pine woods and surrounded by stunning scenery.

On scorching summer days, the cool shade that the trees give is particularly welcome. If you're seeking a peaceful hidden bay in Split, this natural beach is ideal since it is rarely too busy even during the busiest months.

The required food and beverages are also available at a neighboring restaurant. Bene Beach can only be accessed on foot, by bicycle, or by bus number 12 since a section of the park is off-limits to vehicles. Throughout the summer, a tiny, slow train also runs to this beach.

SPLIT FOR FAMILIES

Family-Friendly Activities

You're wondering what to do with your kids in Split, good news Split is a wonderful city for families with small children! Making your Split or Dalmatian Islands vacation activities as entertaining, easy, and educational as possible will keep the kids active and engaged, depending on the age of your child (children). The following are some family-friendly things to do in Split:

Touring by Foot

One of the essential kid-friendly activities to discover this 1700-year-old town is a trip to the Diocletian Palace in Split. Take the youngsters up to the bell tower of the Cathedral of St. Duje if they are not too little.

Bring them to the statue of Grgur Ninski, who is seen wiping his thumb and wishing.

Cycling

Renting a bike in Split is the perfect way to take in the Diocletian Palace, Marjan Hill, or a trip to one of the city's most well-liked beaches.

To avoid fatigue at the conclusion of the journey, you may hire an electric bike for little children or request extra kid seats. Inquire at a nearby Split bike rental shop about costs and further details.

Go to the Klis Fort

When choosing the finest kid-friendly activities for the entire family, visiting the nearby renowned Klis fortification is a worthwhile excursion.

Kids will love exploring this old military building and museum, where they can view a variety of weapons, armor, and traditional clothing.

If you are driving, it is just 5 miles from Split to Sinj town. capture local bus number 22 from the National Theater bus station and numbers 35 and 36 from the bus station Sukoisanska to go to this stronghold, from where you can capture some stunning panoramic photos of Split and the islands.

The stronghold is open every day from 10 till 16, except Mondays, and admission is 20 kn for adults and 10 kn for children.

Marjan Hill Park

When you first arrive in Split, the ancient city is dominated by a green hill in the distance. Marjan Hill is a natural urban oasis and a popular spot for family outings.

The park has playgrounds, natural trails, scenic views, bird viewing opportunities, and the Split zoo.

Visit Carobni Grad, the Magic City of Split.

At the Poljud Stadium, there is a large indoor play area called Carobni Grad (Magical City). The ideal location, particularly when the weather is bad.

Your child may choose from a wide variety of kid-friendly activities after enrolling, each of which is held in a large playroom furnished with a different theme: a pirate assault, a soccer field, a dolls home, a kitchen, a climbing structure, 2 levels of genuine kid-fun!

Day tour to Vis - Blue Cave from Split

I recommend taking a one-day boat trip to the island of Vis and the well-known Blue Cave to add variety to your kids' activities.

Regular ferries from Split do not run on this route; instead, organized boat excursions that include Hvar Island are the only way to make this journey.

About five kilometers to the southwest of Vis island the 5.8-square-kilometer Bisevo island is where you'll find Blue Cave. While the remainder of the island is covered with macchia or rocks, the center is a fruitful field.

On the island, there are a few caves, the most well-known of which is Modra Spilja.

When the sea is calm around midday, sunbeams that enter through the underwater aperture in the cave reflect off of the white bottom floor and give the cave a blue hue while giving silver to things in the water.

Since 1884, it has been possible to enter the cave, but only by boat. The fishing is excellent along the shore.

The island of Bisevo is a well-known destination for excursions; one-day trips are scheduled from Vis and Komiza as well as other nearby islands.

You visit the Blue Cave first, then go swimming in one of the coves, and then you have a delicious fish meal.

Picigin Game

A popular beach in Split that has received a Blue flag is Bacvice. Families will be enthralled by a recreation area that has several kid-friendly amenities including slides, a trampoline, and a rubber castle.

The beach is a family-friendly and secure location. Additionally, it is the closest beach to Split's ferry port and city center.

The only area where youngsters may observe the popular picigin game or even practice because the water is shallow and they don't require jelly shoes is on this sandy beach! The game's rules are quite basic.

Children's Submarine Activities

This year, a new tour has been added to the Split kids' activities. For families with children, Split always has something fresh to offer. A new tour using a little red semi-submarine has just been presented from Split's seaside "Riva promenade."

A day trip with the Marijeta submarine firm lasts around 45 minutes, while a night excursion is just 30 minutes long. For adults and kids of all ages, this unusual watercraft provides a fun and secure excursion.

While its hull, the underwater observatory, is 1.5 meters (5 feet) below the surface, it is always above sea level. There is a wealth of marine life that you may see via your own private viewing glass.

You may also take in the breathtaking view of the ancient complex of Split with the Palace of Diocletian as you are always free to leave the cabin and go for a stroll on the deck.

$15 is the cost for a single person, although discounts for large families may be available.

SPLIT FOR COUPLES

Romantic Activities and Experiences

Split is a fascinating and romantic location for couples seeking to have a special vacation together. Here are some romantic things to do and places to go with your significant other in Split, from meandering through old alleyways to having supper by the sea at sunset:

Take A Love-Inspiring Picnic

Long a favorite weekend destination for residents and guests of the seaside city, Marjan Forest Park. The expansive nature reserve towers 178 meters above Marjan Hill and is covered in a thick Mediterranean pine forest. Beautiful native flora and wildlife may be seen from the uncommon vantage points that overlook the whole city and its neighboring gorgeous islands.

If you're feeling energetic, there are tennis courts where you can play a game of "love to thirty" with your significant other as well as hiking and running routes that loop through the picturesque terrain. A zoo and a botanical garden are also included in the park.

Bring a delectable picnic, and after a two-hour trek to the top of the hill, you'll have found the ideal location for a private lunch with a breathtaking view.

Escape the Crowds

The best location for romance and leisure is a stunning beach. Couples seeking solitude choose Kastelet Beach, which is located on the south side of the steep Marjan peninsula, whereas residents often favor the urban Bavice Beach.

Wide and fine-pebbled Kastelet Beach has shallow banks where you may simply wade in to cool yourself. The sun-kissed beach provides little shade, making it perfect for top-up tanning. Although you may hire sun loungers, if you want to unwind in the shade, you'll need to bring your own parasol. However, there are showers, toilets, and changing rooms accessible, as well as a beach bar right on the property.

Share Your Tasting Adventure

Couples may satisfy their senses and palates by partaking in a wine-tasting excursion in Split. You will be introduced to a few of the best wines made in the Dalmatian area by a trained sommelier.

You may discover everything about the development of Croatian wine culture and the methods used to make wine while you drink a glass of powerful red or crisp white wine and look into the eyes of your special someone. Additionally, you'll get to try out a range of delectable treats that go well together.

Visit the vibrant Peskarija (fish market) and Pazar (green market) as part of a culinary tour of Split, and stock up on fresh ingredients for a fancy meal.

Enjoy A Sunset Seduction

Slowly, the sun falls over the Adriatic Sea's sparkling turquoise horizon, changing the pristine sky's lovely soft blue tones in favor of warm golden orange and red tint. You may take in this breathtaking vista from a special vantage point. Join a kayaking sunset trip with your significant other and take in the breathtaking scenery as paddling around the rocky shoreline of the walled seaside city.

Enjoy Yourself on The Riva Promenade

One of the most significant public areas in Split is the Riva promenade, which runs beside the harbor. The pedestrian area of the Riva promenade, which is located on the south front of the Diocletian Palace, is flanked with trendy tiny cafés and sophisticated restaurants where couples can unwind and take in the romantic ambiance.

The thriving cultural center serves as a premier location for sporting events, seasonal festivals, and carnivals.

It's a good idea to save the evening for some intimacy after a day spent enjoying Split's attractions and joys with your special someone. Enjoy a special evening for two at one of the friendly neighborhood establishments that serves authentic Dalmatian and Croatian food. Share a tray of delicious local treats and a few glasses of wine produced nearby. The majority of the city's restaurants also include traditional meals with Mediterranean, Austrian, Hungarian, and Turkish influences on their menus.

Finish off the ideal evening by enjoying vibrant drinks at a chic bar on the seafront. You can always live it up and flaunt your finest moves on the dance floor at one of the neighborhood's throbbing nightclubs till the wee hours of the following day if you don't want your love rendezvous to end.

Cruise to Nearby Islands

Set sail towards adjacent islands like Hvar or Bra. Take in the Adriatic's splendor while traveling along the picturesque route and exploring the quaint settlements.

Sunset Sail

Rent a private sailing vessel and take in a sunset sail off Split's shore. Watching the sun go behind the horizon is lovely.

Couples Massage and Spa Day

Indulge in a revitalizing spa day at one of the city's opulent wellness facilities with a couples massage or other restorative services.

Stargazing at Night

To enjoy stargazing at night, go to a less populated section of Marjan Hill. The serene environment and blue sky make for a lovely scene.

SHOPPING AND DINING

Local Cuisine and Specialties

Split has a wonderful selection of regional foods and delicacies that are guaranteed to tempt your palate. The Mediterranean influences, fresh ingredients, and age-old traditions are profoundly ingrained in the city's culinary culture. Here are some regional delicacies and foods you just must eat when in Split:

Buzara

Buzara is a white wine-based shellfish stew popular in Croatia. Although it is often cooked with shrimp, it may also be found with other seafood, like as crab or lobster. Bread is provided with the meal so that you may savor the exquisite sauce to its fullest.

Many eateries in the area include buzara on their menus. It's the ideal approach to take advantage of the amazing seafood harvest on the Dalmatian coast.

Crni Rizot

Crni rizot is a rice dish that is dyed a stunning shade of black using squid ink. Although shellfish is used most often, you may also find chicken or sausage in certain variations of the meal. It's a substantial meal that's ideal for a chilly winter day, and your friends back home will be impressed by the dish's unusual hue.

If you like shellfish, crni rizot is another excellent choice since it's often served with seafood like mussels and clams. You may be able to locate a vegetarian version of this traditional dish, however, if you seek around.

Peka

A sort of stew made with meat or vegetables called peka is prepared in an underground oven. It is a common meal in Croatia, however, you may also find variants cooked with chicken, octopus, or veal. The beef is exceptionally soft and flavorful since the meal is slow-cooked.

Typically eaten with potatoes, peka is a full and hearty dish. You can get it at several eateries across the city, and it's the ideal way to stay warm on a chilly day. Just be sure you order it ahead of time since it needs time to cook. The dish is traditionally prepared behind a bell-shaped iron or terra cotta cover. Even while it's not precisely quick food, these meals are nevertheless rather tasty.

Pasticada

Popular in Dalmatian cooking is stewed beef known as pasticada. The meal is often served with gnocchi or pasta and is produced by simmering meat in a tomato sauce. The extended cooking period makes the beef exceptionally soft and tasty. It's a hearty meal that will keep you energized for exploring all day.

Many restaurants in Spilt provide pasticada, which is often accompanied by typical Croatian sides like potatoes or cabbage.

On a sweltering day, pasticada may not be the ideal option for cooling yourself. Additionally, it's definitely not the healthiest meal available, so if you're trying to limit your calorie consumption, you should probably steer clear of it.

But this is a terrific option if all you want is a good traditional supper.

Sarma

Spilt residents often eat sarma, a sort of stuffed cabbage meal. A tomato sauce is used to cook the filled cabbage leaves, which are produced by stuffing them with ground beef and rice.

The longevity of this meal, with its origins in the Ottoman Empire, is a tribute to how good it is. Additionally well-liked in the surrounding nations of Montenegro, Bosnia, Bulgaria, and Romania are these filled cabbage rolls.

In Split, sarma is a common item on menus and is often accompanied by typical Croatian sides like potatoes or bread.

Brodetto

Fish stews like brodetto are popular in Dalmatian cooking. It's prepared by simmering fish and shellfish in a tomato sauce, and it's often served with bread so you can savor every last bite.

Brodetto is readily available on the menus of eateries in Split. This is particularly true if you go down near the lake, where you can get some of the tastiest and freshest seafood in the whole city.

Pršut

A form of cured ham known as prut is dry-cured with salt and spices before being matured for a number of months. This procedure provides the ham with a distinctive taste that makes it ideal for thinly slicing for solo consumption. Put some carbohydrates on a couple of pieces of bread if your meal calls for them, and you're set to go.

Prut may be found at many local eateries and is often offered as an appetizer or side dish. Additionally, it's a typical component in a few of Split's traditional foods, like sarma and pasticada.

Krostule Fritters

Krostule fritters are a kind of pastry that are often served as a dessert or a snack. They are produced by frying dough in oil. They may be served plain or with fruit inside, and before serving, they are often coated with sugar.

Krostule is a delectable and sweet dish that can be found in many of Split's eateries and cafés. They are highly addicting, so be aware that it's simple to consume much more than you meant.

Baklava

This common treat cannot be attributed to Croatia. One of the most popular baked pastries consumed across the whole Mediterranean region, numerous nations claim to have developed it.

But regardless of where it originates, Split has several fantastic examples of baklava, including those that use regional ingredients. Again, this is not the healthiest dinner in the world, but it is delicious and perfect for takeaway. Baklava is created by stacking thin pastry sheets with nuts and honey and baking them until they are flaky and golden brown. Consider yourself forewarned—it's often quite sweet.

A common flatbread found in many Mediterranean cuisines is called **Pita**. The dough is cooked in oil to create the bread, which is often offered as a side dish or snack. It may be eaten with a fork and knife and can be simple or loaded with shredded cheese or meat.

Pita is so common that you can get it almost everywhere. It often occurs in fast cuisines, such as kebabs and other grab-and-go dishes, and is frequently served as a side dish to a larger meal.

Rozata

Custard puddings, such as rozata, are common in Dalmatian cooking. Eggs, milk, and sugar are cooked together until they are thick and creamy to make the pudding. It's often served as a dessert and is frequently flavored with vanilla or lemon. Just be aware that it's pretty rich and simple to eat in excessive amounts.

Boskarin

In the restaurants in Split, you may often encounter a sort of beef called boskarin. The meat originates from local farms' famous long-horned Istrian cow. The beef is matured for a number of months after being dry-cured with salt and spices. Due to this procedure, the beef has a distinctive taste that makes it ideal for thinly slicing and eating on its own or as part of a charcuterie dish.

Usually served as an appetizer or side dish, this meaty meal is. As an alternative, you may purchase it in a sandwich, however, purists would object to doing so. To experience this special Dalmatian delicacy, try it as a carpaccio, with spaghetti, or in boskarin tail soup. Nothing is more regional than this.

Grilled Seafood

One of the best foods to eat in Split is grilled fish, which is common in Dalmatian cooking. Due to the city's proximity to the Adriatic Sea, fresh fish and seafood are always available. Additionally, the Dalmatians are experts at grilling.

You must taste grilled fish in the city; it is often served as a main meal. Just know that it may be pretty pricey, so you might not want to eat it every day. However, grilled fish is absolutely worth spending on if you're looking for pleasure.

Popular Restaurants and Cafes

Konoba Hvaranin

The Hvaranin, owned by the Radovani family, is one of Split's classic establishments and was formerly a dull café. This is a second home for many journalists and authors whose books are displayed, with mom and dad in the kitchen and son behind the bar. Everything is straightforward, homemade, and delicious.

The Hvar-style gregada fish stew and the white risotto with mussels are specialties. Don't forget to indulge in the classic dessert, roata crème caramel. Booking in advance is advised due to limited seating.

Konoba Fetivi

A true jewel of Dalmatia, Konoba Fetivi is a casual dining establishment that honors and respects the region's abundant foodstuffs by putting them center stage. The restaurant is run by a family that has lived in the area for 300 years and serves regional specialties, including several meat dishes, but the seafood is the star of the menu. The seafood menu (as well as certain items like the shared seafood platter) changes every day depending on the season and what has been caught.

The flavors of the seafood are kept to the usual salt, pepper, lemon, fresh garlic, and sumptuously delicious olive oil, which is served in little bottles on each table. The seafood is prepared simply and grilled to perfection.

Bokamorra

Although Bokamorra has a large glass façade that enables diners to take advantage of the vistas, the restaurant's attractive interior and the excellent pizza and martini presentation are more than enough to keep customers interested. They only provide pizza, along with a dessert choice, but fortunately, theirs are the finest in town.

A delectable pizza foundation is produced with dough that has been matured for 48 hours, and it is topped with premium toppings including cheeses, truffles, salad greens, and air-dried meats. Although your granny may object to the loud level, the seating is funky, the booths are perfect for groups, including kids, and the youthful crowd is kept engaged by terrific music (sometimes even a DJ).

Konoba Marjan

This little, family-run restaurant with a checkered tablecloth in the center of the Varo district has long been a favorite among the locals. Almost all of the seafood options from the Adriatic are available here, including grilled fresh fish, seafood risottos, scampi, and squid.

Additionally, you may enjoy traditional Dalmatian food there, such as paticada, a well-known regional stew prepared from meat that has been marinated in wine and prunes.

Apetit

On the western edge of Diocletian's Palace, next to the Riva, this wonderful new enterprise from a Croatian who spent many years in Berlin shares a historic structure that has been tastefully renovated. This is a terrific location for an upscale lunch because of the green dividers, stone walls, vibrant artwork, and modest furniture.

In addition to a vegetable section and lots of options for meat and fish eaters, the typical Dalmatian cuisine includes homemade ingredients like pasta and bread. Add homemade chocolate cake to finish.

Trattoria Tinel

The entrance to the Varo quarter's expanding restaurant district is gradually transforming the neighborhood into one of Split's most popular eating districts. With seafood risottos and pastas in the 50kn range and more costly items like scampi and lobster on the menu, the newest addition

Tinel is another restaurant that aims to provide high-quality Dalmatian cuisine at reasonable costs.

The restaurant's décor is pleasantly tidy and bright and avoids the traditional Dalmatian stereotypes. It also offers a cozy outdoor patio at the rear.

Brasserie on 7

As a kind of continuation of the previously successful Zinfandel, Brasserie on 7 shares ownership and a similar guiding principle. In the center of the city's principal beachfront promenade, Riva, it has one of the most central sites. With a wonderful assortment of reimagined local and foreign cuisine, this restaurant quickly rose to become one of the rising stars of Split's culinary scene.

Highlights include the chilled seafood platter, smoked salmon, or octopus salad on the fish side; for visitors who prefer meat, there is also a Black Angus burger with pancetta and Portobello mushrooms or a lamb leg with rosemary and yogurt.

NoStress Bistro

The position of NoStress, which is in the center of the busiest area of Split's main plaza, is hard to top. A tourist trap should be the ideal location here. NoStress, however, is not like that. Since proprietors Ana and Eljko Alfirevi engaged seasoned chef Eljko Neven Bremec, NoStress has become one of the city's most cutting-edge restaurants.

The majority of its food is produced using local resources, with seasonal specialties that change often, such as wild asparagus in the spring and homemade sausages in the winter.

Mazzgoon

Young newlyweds Sara and Toni Vrsalovi are the proprietors of another modest but potent bastion of Split's emerging culinary scene. It is situated exactly opposite the Diocletian Palace's Iron or Western Gate, which was intended to be utilized by the imperial guard of Rome. Now, in the garden of a historic castle in Split, there is this contemporary indoor area next to a shaded and comfortable patio.

The term Mazzgoon is derived from the Dalmatian word for mule, Mazga, which is renowned for its unwavering perseverance. Additionally, its food combines regional specialties with influences from elsewhere.

Korta

One of the popular sites in Split's Palace district is Poljana Grgura Ninskog, a little enclosed piazza that almost has the sense of a private courtyard. It is off-limits to visitors but often used by residents traveling from Silver Gate to Golden Gate.

One corner of the plaza formerly housed the trendy bar Planet Jazz; now, Korta, a tranquil restaurant that combines Dalmatian history with contemporary culinary flair, has taken over that location. The ratio of fish to beef to pasta on the menu is just right. San Servolo, a great beer produced by a small brewery in Istria, is only available in a select few locations in Split, including Korta.

Boban

The best gastronomy guides in Croatia commend Boban, which was established in 1973 and is located a short distance from Firule amid residential structures; the cab driver will be aware of it.

The restaurant's specialties include pancetta-wrapped monkfish fillets served over rice with a cream sauce, home-made gnocchi packed with scampi and prosciutto, and filet mignon in a red wine and truffle sauce. Count on the finest regional wines.

Kadena

The Kadena has the same expansive terrace as the previous Bekan and offers stunning views of Zenta Marina and the far-off islands. The dishes on the tasting menus range in price from 270 to 320 won.

The wine selection calls for a sizable cellar. A variety of bruschette and inventive desserts are added to a traditional Dalmatian meal that has already been given a new depth by the innovative use of new ingredients and sauces.

Shopping Districts and Markets

Diocletian's Palace Market (Pazar):

At the heart of Split lies the historic Diocletian's Palace, a UNESCO World Heritage Site that houses an enchanting market known as "Pazar." This bustling marketplace comes alive with an assortment of stalls offering an assortment of fruits, vegetables, and fresh produce, along with an array of local products, spices, and traditional Croatian delights.

Pazar is an ideal destination to immerse oneself in the city's authentic ambiance and sample local flavors.

Green Market (Pazar Plinarska

Adjacent to the aforementioned Diocletian's Palace Market, the Green Market is a must-visit for those in search of the freshest ingredients. Here, vendors present a colorful array of seasonal fruits, vegetables, herbs, cheeses, and more. The market's jovial atmosphere provides a genuine glimpse into local life as shoppers mingle and engage with vendors.

Marmont Street and Peristil Square:

Marmont Street, a bustling pedestrian thoroughfare, is adorned with an array of boutiques, fashion stores, and gift shops, catering to both fashion enthusiasts and those seeking unique souvenirs. As you amble along, you'll discover an eclectic mix of international brands and local designer boutiques. Adjacent to Marmont Street, the charismatic Peristil Square features stalls selling artisanal crafts, jewelry, and traditional Croatian products.

Fruit Square (Voćni trg):

Nestled within the confines of Diocletian's Palace, the Fruit Square emanates a captivating charm. Its name is a nod to its historical role as a market for fruits, but it has now transformed into a bustling spot featuring cafes, restaurants, and shops. This area is a remarkable blend of old and new, seamlessly marrying antiquity with contemporary commerce.

Mall of Split (City Center One Split):

For those who crave a modern shopping experience, the Mall of Split, also known as City Center One Split, is a prime destination. Located a short distance from the city center, this expansive mall boasts a plethora of international and domestic brands, a multiplex cinema, dining options, and entertainment facilities. It is a hub of convenience that caters to various shopping and leisure preferences.

Bokeria Market:

Bokeria Market, also known as "Fish Market" or "Ribarnica," is a vibrant hub for seafood enthusiasts. Situated near the waterfront, this market is a seafood lover's paradise, offering an impressive selection of fresh fish, shellfish, and other aquatic delights. The market exudes a lively atmosphere as vendors skillfully display their catch of the day, creating a sensory experience that immerses visitors in the maritime culture of the region.

Artisan Workshops and Galleries:

Split's shopping scene extends beyond traditional markets and commercial centers to encompass a variety of artisan workshops and galleries. Wander through the winding streets of the old town to discover workshops where local craftsmen create handcrafted leather goods, ceramics, jewelry, and intricate lacework. These establishments provide a window into the city's artistic heritage and offer visitors the opportunity to procure unique, locally-made treasures.

Old Town Boutiques:

As you meander through Split's charming Old Town, you'll encounter an assortment of boutiques that cater to discerning shoppers. These boutiques curate an array of high-quality clothing, accessories, and home decor, often featuring designs influenced by local culture and trends.

The Old Town's narrow alleyways reveal hidden gems where fashion enthusiasts can discover pieces that reflect both contemporary styles and historical aesthetics.

Antique and Vintage Shops:

For those with a penchant for antiquities and vintage finds, Split has a selection of shops that cater to this refined taste. These establishments showcase an array of unique items, including vintage clothing, collectibles, artworks, and artifacts.

Exploring these shops not only presents the opportunity to acquire one-of-a-kind pieces but also offers a glimpse into the city's past through its carefully curated treasures.

Specialty Food Stores:

Delve into the world of Croatian gastronomy by exploring specialty food stores scattered across Split. These establishments stock an array of local delicacies such as olive oil, wines, cheeses, cured meats, and truffle products. Not only can you indulge in these delectable offerings during your visit, but you can also bring a piece of the region's culinary heritage home with you.

Souvenirs and Local Products

Exploring the local souvenirs and products in Split offers an immersive way to connect with the city's culture and heritage. Here's a detailed overview of some of the delightful items you can consider purchasing during your visit:

Olive Oil:

Croatia is renowned for its high-quality olive oil, and Split is no exception. You'll find an array of locally-produced olive oils that showcase the region's rich agricultural heritage. Look for bottles labeled with designations such as "extra virgin" and "cold-pressed" to ensure you're getting the finest quality.

Wines and Spirits:

Croatia boasts a burgeoning wine scene, and Split is a fantastic place to explore local wines. Look for indigenous grape varieties such as Plavac Mali and Pošip. Dingač and Plavac are popular red wines, while Grk and Pošip are well-regarded white wines. For something stronger, consider purchasing local spirits like rakija, a traditional fruit brandy.

Lavender Products:

Lavender is a symbol of the Dalmatian coast, and you'll find an array of lavender-based products in Split. These include aromatic sachets, essential oils, soaps, and even culinary products like lavender-infused honey. These products capture the soothing essence of the region.

Traditional Croatian Sweets:

Treat yourself to traditional Croatian sweets like "fritule," small deep-fried doughnuts often flavored with citrus zest and sometimes filled with raisins or chocolate chips. You can also find "rozata," a caramelized custard dessert, and various fruit preserves that showcase local flavors.

Ceramics and Pottery:

The city is dotted with workshops offering exquisite ceramics and pottery. From intricately hand-painted plates and bowls to unique decorative pieces, these items reflect the artistic spirit of Split and make for elegant keepsakes.

Dalmatian Fig Products:

Dalmatian figs are a regional specialty, and you can find them in various forms, from dried figs to fig jams and spreads. These products capture the sweetness of the Adriatic climate and offer a delicious taste of local flavors.

Traditional Croatian Textiles and Lace:

Croatian lacework, especially from the town of Pag, is known for its intricate patterns and delicate craftsmanship. Look for tablecloths, doilies, and decorative items made from this traditional craft.

Salt from Nin:

The town of Nin, near Split, is renowned for its salt production. Consider purchasing sea salt products such as flavored salts, bath salts, and even skincare products infused with the beneficial properties of salt.

Handmade Jewelry and Accessories:

Local artisans craft unique jewelry pieces inspired by the region's history and culture. Look for items made from silver, semi-precious stones, and other local materials.

Traditional Attire and Embroidery:

If you're looking for something truly authentic, consider purchasing traditional Croatian attire like a "kaftan" or "fustanella" for men, or embroidered blouses and dresses for women. These items are a testament to the city's cultural heritage.

Dalmatian Prosciutto and Cheese:

Indulge in the flavors of Dalmatia by bringing home slices of locally-cured prosciutto and artisanal cheeses. The region's unique climate contributes to the exceptional taste of these products, making them a delectable souvenir for food enthusiasts.

Traditional Musical Instruments:

For those intrigued by Croatian folk music, consider acquiring a traditional musical instrument such as the "tamburica," a stringed instrument central to the country's musical heritage. These instruments serve as not only souvenirs but also as unique conversation pieces.

Nautical and Maritime-Themed Souvenirs:

Given Split's coastal location, you'll find an array of nautical-inspired souvenirs. Look for items like sailor's knots, ship models, and maritime-themed textiles that pay homage to the city's deep connection with the sea.

Local Artwork and Prints:

Explore galleries and boutiques to discover local artwork, prints, and photography that capture the essence of Split's landscapes, architecture, and culture. These pieces can serve as a lasting memory of your journey and add a touch of elegance to your home.

Authentic Filigree Jewelry:

Filigree jewelry is a traditional craft that involves intricate metalwork. In Split, you'll find artisans who create stunning filigree pieces, including earrings, necklaces, and bracelets, reflecting the city's artisanal heritage.

Adriatic Coral Jewelry:

Coral harvesting is a long-standing tradition in the Adriatic Sea, and you can find beautifully-crafted coral jewelry in Split. From necklaces to earrings, these pieces feature vibrant hues and intricate designs.

Handwoven Textiles:

Discover handwoven textiles such as tablecloths, napkins, and shawls that showcase the city's weaving traditions. These items often feature colorful patterns and designs inspired by the surrounding nature and cultural motifs.

Local Cookbooks and Culinary Products:

Bring the flavors of Split into your kitchen by purchasing local cookbooks that feature traditional Croatian recipes. You can also find culinary products like truffle-infused oils, seafood sauces, and spice blends to recreate Dalmatian dishes at home.

Personal Care Products with Mediterranean Ingredients:

Explore stores offering personal care products enriched with Mediterranean ingredients like olive oil, lavender, and herbs. These items, including soaps, lotions, and skincare products, provide a touch of relaxation and luxury.

Traditional Wooden Toys:

If you're looking for gifts for children, traditional wooden toys handcrafted by local artisans offer a touch of nostalgia and authenticity. These toys often reflect local culture and creativity.

As you embark on your journey to explore the souvenirs and local products of Split, remember that each item tells a story of the city's history, culture, and craftsmanship. These mementos serve as tangible connections to your experiences in Split and offer a lasting reminder of the unique charm that defines this Croatian gem.

How to Get the Best Shopping Deals

Securing the best deals while shopping in Split requires a combination of savvy tactics and a respectful approach. Below, you'll find some suggestions to maximize the value of your money:

Compare Prices:

Before making a purchase, take the time to compare prices for similar items across different shops or markets. This will give you an idea of the average price range, helping you identify whether a particular offer is a good deal or not.

Shop Around:

Don't settle for the first shop you encounter. Explore different areas of the city, including both touristy and local districts. Often, prices may vary based on the location and type of shop.

Engage in Polite Bargaining:

Bargaining is a cultural norm in many markets and smaller shops in Split. Politely negotiate the price, keeping in mind that a friendly and respectful attitude goes a long way. Start with a counteroffer that's lower than the original price, and be prepared for some back-and-forth until you reach a mutually acceptable price.

Buy in Bulk:

If you're interested in purchasing multiple items from the same shop, inquire about discounts for buying in bulk.

Some shopkeepers may be open to offering you a better price if you're buying more than one item.

Shop During Off-Peak Hours:

Shopping during quieter times, such as early mornings or late afternoons, can work in your favor. Shopkeepers may be more willing to negotiate prices when there are fewer customers around.

Build a Rapport:

Engage in friendly conversation with the shopkeepers, ask about their products, and express genuine interest in their offerings. Building a rapport can make them more inclined to offer you a good deal.

Be Mindful of Quality:

While searching for deals, don't compromise on quality. Ensure that the items you're purchasing are well-made and authentic. It's better to pay a bit more for a high-quality item than to buy something of subpar quality at a lower price.

Check for Package Deals:

Some shops may offer package deals or discounts if you purchase multiple related items. For example, if you're buying clothing, inquire about potential discounts for buying a matching set or multiple pieces.

Ask Locals for Recommendations:

Locals often have insights into the best places to shop and where you can find quality items at reasonable prices. Feel free to seek advice from hotel staff, tour guides, or amiable locals you encounter.

Research Local Customs:

Research local customs and etiquette related to shopping and bargaining. Understanding cultural norms can help you navigate the shopping experience more effectively.

Consider Cash Payment:

Some shopkeepers may offer a small discount if you pay in cash, as it saves them credit card processing fees. However, make sure to have the local currency on hand.

Remember that the goal is to strike a balance between securing a good deal and showing respect to the local vendors. Approach bargaining with a positive attitude, and even if you don't get the price you hoped for, the experience of interacting with the local shopkeepers and exploring their offerings is a valuable part of the journey.

NIGHTLIFE IN SPLIT

Split has a lot to offer nightlife aficionados, even if it is mostly recognized for its extensive culture and history. The nightlife in Split provides a wealth of chances to mingle, drink, dance, and most importantly, have fun. The city is brimming with festive cheer!

Split's nightlife is thriving and varied every day of the week in the summer. The nightlife in the Croatian city mostly takes place outside and features open-air performances, festivals, clubs, and eateries.

The main nightlife areas in Split are:

Riva: This is the main seafront promenade in Split, and it is lined with bars and restaurants. It is a great place to start your night with a drink and some people-watching.

Diocletian's Palace: This ancient palace is home to some of Split's most popular bars and clubs. The narrow streets and hidden courtyards of the palace make for a fun and atmospheric place to party.

Bacvice Beach: This beach is a popular spot for swimming and sunbathing during the day, but it transforms into a party destination at night. There are several bars and clubs on the beach, and the party atmosphere is contagious.

On weekdays, bars in the old center often remain open until midnight, and on weekends, until 2am. The celebration goes to Split's other nightclubs and discos when the old town's taverns shut.

Nightclubs in Split don't open until after 11:00 p.m. and become busy until 1:00 a.m., when the old town's taverns start to shut down. The last nightclubs close around five in the morning.

The majority of Split's pubs and clubs are located in and around the city center, so getting around is easy and everything is close at hand.

Best Bars and Nightclubs

<u>CLUBS</u>

Mandrach Night Club

Operating daily from 8:00 AM to 12:00 AM.

The Mandrach nightclub situated in Split offers top-tier entertainment, complete with a team comprising DJs, dancers, singers, and a staff dedicated to ensuring a vibrant party ambiance and flawless service. Sunset, music, scenic ocean vistas, cocktails, and a convivial environment are just a few of the facets to discover.

In addition to a diverse assortment of beverages, the Mandrach restaurant also caters to all palates with its superb cuisine, ranging from mouthwatering burgers and succulent steaks to delectable fish specialties.

Central Club

Ranked among the finest nightclubs in Split, Central Club is a dazzling and glamorous venue highly favored by tourists, delivering all the requisites for a night of revelry in Split. Spanning two floors with four bars, VIP lounges, and a striking dance floor, the club hosts international DJs and local Croatian stars nightly, with music encompassing club classics, hip hop, RnB, and the latest dance chart-toppers.

Vanilla Club

Open on Fridays and Saturdays from 11:00 PM to 5:00 AM.

Situated behind the Poljud stadium at a short distance from the historic center, Vanilla Club stands out as one of Split's most bustling nightspots. The club consistently draws crowds during the summer months, and the spacious terrace invariably offers a quiet spot to savor a cocktail.

Throughout the summer season, a plethora of live concerts and DJ performances fill the regular parties with commercial tunes. Dress smartly.

Caffe-Club Bačvice

Operating daily from 9:00 AM to 4:00 AM.

Nestled along Bacvice Beach, Caffe-Club Bacvice holds a prominent spot as a sought-after nightclub in Split. Positioned on the waterfront, the club boasts breathtaking ocean panoramas. It's a trendy destination to impress and dance the night away in Split.

Academia Club Ghetto

Open from Monday to Friday, 6:00 PM to 12:00 AM, and Saturday to Sunday, 6:00 PM to 1:00 AM.

Located within a courtyard in the Old Town district, Academia Club Ghetto transcends the typical definition of a Split nightclub, doubling as an art gallery and a gathering place for artists and travelers alike. Unwind in the charming courtyard area before exploring the art-adorned chambers and dancing into the night. With reasonably priced beers and wines, it's a fun venue for a serene night out. Live bands often take the stage, fostering an underground club atmosphere.

Jazzbina

Open on Fridays and Saturdays from 8:00 PM to 3:00 AM. Positioned at the commencement of Sinjska Street, Jazzbina ranks as one of Split's most favored nightclubs. Tall tables and chairs, coupled with an extensive selection of domestic and imported beers, conjure an Irish ambiance. The musical repertoire predominantly harks back to the 90s, making this establishment a must-visit for those nostalgically inclined toward older melodies.

Fabrique Pub

Operating hours are Sunday to Wednesday from 10:00 AM to 12:00 AM, Thursday from 10:00 AM to 1:00 AM, and Friday and Saturday from 10:00 AM to 2:00 AM.

Situated at the western tip of the Riva promenade, Fabrique Pub stands as a highly frequented disco bar, particularly adored by tourists, especially in the summer months. The establishment boasts an attractive industrial-style interior and boasts a selection of over 40 international beers. The venue is spacious, featuring a front room dedicated to beverages and a rear room designed for dining.

Fabrique remains open until 2:00 AM, offering a platform for DJs and live bands to entertain patrons during the weekends. It has become a hallmark of Split's nightlife scene.

InBOX Bar

Positioned by the ferry port, InBOX ranks among the largest bars and nightclubs in Split, renowned for hosting some of the city's most exuberant parties. It holds considerable popularity among young tourists and is a key stop on the renowned Split bar tours.

Moon bar

Operating hours are Sunday to Thursday from 7:00 AM to 12:00 AM, and Friday and Saturday from 7:00 AM to 3:00 AM.

Moon Bar has swiftly ascended the ranks to become one of Split's most favored nightclubs. With an array of themed nights and a roster of DJs and live bands performing throughout the year, the venue is always alive with activity. The modern and futuristic interior design significantly contributes to the ambiance. While it might occasionally get crowded, this factor only enhances the overall mood.

Gooshter Beach Club

Positioned beyond Split's city center, Gooshter stands as a sophisticated and elegant beach club integrated into a 5-star hotel complex. The club boasts a remarkably crafted design, featuring rustic woven fronds that provide daytime shade and create a welcoming ambiance through nighttime illumination.

Visit to indulge in sunset vibes and breathtaking ocean vistas. The club maintains a tranquil atmosphere during most nights, partly due to its relatively early closing times.

BARS

Antique Bar

Operating hours are from 8:00 AM to 2:00 AM, seven days a week.

Nestled along the Riva promenade, Antique Bar seamlessly melds classic design with contemporary allure. An air of hedonism hangs in the atmosphere, making it an ideal spot to unwind over coffee or a well-crafted drink. The evenings witness bustling crowds and a delightful musical backdrop.

ST-Riva Cocktail Bar

Open Sunday to Thursday from 7:00 AM to 12:00 AM, and Friday and Saturday from 7:00 AM to 2:00 AM.

Situated by the waterfront on the southern side of Diocletian's Palace, ST-Riva ranks as one of Split's liveliest bars during early evening hours. While tables and chairs grace the promenade like its counterparts, the real charm lies in the balcony on the first floor, offering a vantage point over the Riva.

The Riva remains bustling all year, but truly comes alive during the summer months, when the thoroughfare thrives with festivals, street performers, curious tourists, and locals.

The Daltonist Craft Bar

Open Sunday to Wednesday from 10:00 AM to 12:00 AM, and Thursday to Saturday from 10:00 AM to 1:00 AM.

The Daltonist stands as a sought-after craft cocktail bar in Split, adorned with charming stone decor. The establishment crafts cocktails inspired by Dalmatian traditions, characterized by their light and refreshing nature. Additionally, a fine selection of craft beers and local brandies grace their menu.

Shotgun Shooters

Operating hours are from 8:00 PM to 2:00 AM, daily.

A delightful little establishment, Shotgun Shooters Bar serves as a fantastic starting point for your party night in Split. The bar exudes energy and boasts an enjoyable atmosphere, complemented by tantalizing yet potent cocktails, all at reasonable prices.

Bar Sistema

Open Tuesday to Saturday from 5:00 PM to 1:00 AM.

Bar Sistema ranks among the finest cocktail bars in Split, exuding an exquisite ambiance with its elongated bar and towering liquor cabinet, akin to a scene from New York.

The signature cocktails are a treat, and the extensive variety of whiskey adds to its allure.

Noor Bar

Open Monday to Saturday from 6:00 PM to 1:00 AM, and Sunday from 6:00 PM to 12:00 AM.

Noor offers a snug and inviting ambiance with an impressive selection of cocktails and spirits. While the interior space is cozy yet limited, it accommodates around 20 patrons at most. During warm summer nights, the front staircase transforms into a charming terrace.

Lvxor

Operating hours are from 8:00 AM to 12:00 AM, every day.

Situated at Peristyle Square, this historical café stands out as one of Split's most unique bars, possibly one of the oldest, attracting a considerable tourist following. Outdoor seating lines the burgundy cushions of the Palazzo staircase, providing a pleasant setting for patrons to enjoy a drink. Come evening, relish the enchanting atmosphere while listening to live performances by talented young Split musicians.

Leopold's Delicatessen Bar

Open Monday to Friday from 8:00 AM to 1:00 AM, and Saturday and Sunday from 8:00 AM to 2:00 AM.

Positioned on Dosud Street, Leopold shines as a prime destination for craft beer enthusiasts. While the bar's interior is cozy albeit compact, outdoor seating on the steps offers an inviting setting. A diverse selection of craft beers, both from their own brew and other breweries, awaits connoisseurs.

ACCOMMODATION OPTIONS

Budget-Friendly Hotels

Exploring Split on a budget doesn't mean compromising on privacy; you can find affordable private accommodations. Here are some of the top choices for budget-conscious travelers seeking economical hotels in Split.

Split Inn Apartments

Nestled in the heart of Split, Split Inn Apartments offer a prime location just a short distance from major city attractions like Diocletian's Palace. These apartments have been praised by previous guests for their boutique-style charm and helpful staff, providing assistance during check-in and aiding in planning your time in Split. Additionally, family rooms are available, with certain apartments featuring terraces for added comfort.

BVB Rooms Split

Solo travelers who have visited BVB Rooms Split have given rave reviews. The apartments are cherished for their optimal location, garden views, and excellent value for money. Equipped with coffee machines, the rooms are conveniently situated within walking distance of many attractions. Guests often highlight the rooms' cleanliness and upkeep.

A&M Apartment and Rooms

A&M Apartment and Rooms have garnered admiration for their convenient location, allowing easy access to many of Split's premier attractions. Solo travelers, in particular, have taken a liking to these apartments due to their privacy, serene garden area, and the peaceful ambiance of the surrounding neighborhood. Despite the apartments' proximity to the city, guests appreciate the tranquility they offer.

Luxury Apartments

Indulging in luxury is effortless in Split. Discover the finest hotels that place you right in the heart of the city, granting easy access to opulence.

Prima Luxury Rooms

Experience a touch of luxury at Prima Luxury Rooms, where guesthouse accommodation seamlessly intertwines with comfort. These rooms cater to your well-being and offer dedicated workspaces, ideal for business travelers or those working remotely.

Begin your day with a complimentary breakfast, relish the modern and invigorating room designs, and embrace the convenience of walking to Split's premier attractions. Notably, the Riva Promenade stands a mere 400 meters away. Families can opt for spacious accommodations, while solo travelers have spoken highly of their experiences.

Palace Suites Heritage Hotel

Immerse yourself in the grandeur of Split's paramount attraction at Palace Suites Heritage Hotel. Adjacent to Diocletian's Palace, a UNESCO World Heritage site that's a must-see on any Split journey, this hotel offers a blend of modern design within a heritage building. Your windows will serenade you with the vibrant sounds of Split's atmosphere, perhaps even echoing the tunes of traditional local music.

Each room boasts spacious beds, Brazilian wood floors, and luxurious amenities, ensuring an opulent stay.

Starlight Luxury Rooms

Starlight Luxury Rooms offers style and luxury in another guesthouse setting. Nestled within a UNESCO-protected building a mere 150 meters away from Diocletian's Palace, another UNESCO site, this guesthouse exudes historical significance alongside modern elegance and a graceful touch of luxury.

Set in a pedestrian zone, noise pollution from cars remains inconsequential. With a 15-minute stroll to the beach, a short 400-meter distance to the promenade, and a plethora of cafes dotting the vicinity, convenience awaits as soon as you step outside.

Other Alternative Accommodation Options

Ćiri Biri Bela Boutique Hostel

Nestled in Split, the Ćiri Biri Bela Boutique Hostel exudes charm and offers a cozy haven for travelers seeking a restful stay. Opting for an 8-bed dorm room secures you a mere 5-minute walk from Diocletian's Palace. Additionally, you'll have the privilege of enjoying a terrace, perfect for mingling with fellow guests while relishing food and beverages in the heart of Split.

En Route Hostel

Situated slightly away from the city center, En Route Hostel stands as an economical choice for accommodation in Split. Personally experienced and appreciated, the hostel offers spacious rooms that maintain a sense of privacy.

Immaculate bathrooms and the provision of privacy curtains enhance the stay, complemented by a sizable common area that facilitates interactions among travelers. A brief 10-minute stroll leads to the city center, and the beach is even closer.

The hostel facilitates tour bookings and ensures convenience with individual reading lights and lockers for each bed. All essential amenities for a comfortable hostel experience are right at your fingertips.

Al Hostel

Drenched in luminance and expansive in design, Al Hostel creates a delightful space for travelers. Particularly suitable for those embarking on a Croatian road trip, the hostel offers the perk of free parking on-site. A bar, restaurant, and shared lounge enhance the experience, adding to the convenience and comfort.

What's more, the hostel boasts a fabulous location, enabling easy access to numerous must-visit attractions, all within walking distance.

BEST TRAVEL RESOURCES

These are the best travel resources I usually use:

SkyScanner: This is my favorite flight search engine of all time. It always appears to discover the greatest rates, and its calendar display shows you when days are the most affordable to travel. It appeals to me since it searches little booking sites that no one else does. Begin all of your flight searches here.

Momodo: This fantastic website searches a wide range of airlines, including several low-cost carriers that bigger sites overlook. While I usually start with Skyscanner, I'll also look at this site to compare costs.

Google Flights: Google Flights allows you to input your departure airport and view flights all around the globe on a map to get the cheapest destination. It's a useful search engine for learning about routes, connections, and prices.

Hostelworld: The market's most user-friendly hostel website, with the greatest inventory, the finest search interface, and the most availability. You may also look for private rooms or dorm beds. I use it for my reservations.

Couchsurfing: This website enables you to stay for free on people's sofas or in their spare rooms. It's a terrific way to save money while meeting locals who can teach you a lot more about a place than a hostel or hotel can. There are also groups on the web where you can organize to meet up for activities in your location.

Booking.com: Booking.com is an excellent resource for low-cost hotels and other forms of lodging. I enjoy how simple its UI is.

Trusted Housesitters: Try house- or pet-sitting for a novel (and free) way to travel. You just care after someone's home and/or pet while they are gone in return for free lodging. It's an excellent choice for long-term travelers and those on a tight budget.

CONCLUSION

In conclusion, the enchanting city of Split stands as a multifaceted gem that captivates travelers with its rich history, vibrant culture, and breathtaking landscapes. As we wrap up this travel guide, we reflect on the myriad experiences that await those who venture into its inviting embrace.

From the moment you step foot on the sun-kissed shores, Split's allure becomes undeniable. The fusion of ancient wonders and modern energy creates an atmosphere that resonates with both history enthusiasts and contemporary explorers. As you stroll along the narrow streets of the Old Town, you're transported back in time, traversing the same paths as Roman emperors did centuries ago. Diocletian's Palace, the centerpiece of this time capsule, leaves an indelible mark on the cityscape, revealing its storied past and the resilience of its people.

Yet, Split is not just a relic of bygone eras; it's a living, breathing organism that thrives with vitality. The bustling markets, animated cafes, and lively promenades blend seamlessly with the ancient structures, forming a harmonious coexistence that defines the city's character. As the sun sets over the Adriatic horizon, the city transforms into a vibrant hub of entertainment, with its bars, nightclubs, and cultural events inviting you to immerse yourself in the city's pulsating nightlife.

Nature enthusiasts are also bestowed with treasures in Split. From the azure waters of its beaches to the lush greenery of Marjan Hill, the city embraces its natural surroundings with open arms. The resplendent landscapes invite you to explore, whether you're hiking along scenic trails, discovering hidden coves, or soaking in the therapeutic waters of the local beaches.

Delving into the city's culinary scene is a journey in itself. The markets overflow with fresh produce, and the restaurants offer a tantalizing array of Dalmatian dishes that reflect both tradition and innovation. Sampling local delicacies, paired with a glass of Croatian wine, becomes an experience that engages all the senses.

Moreover, the warmth and hospitality of the locals infuse every corner of Split. Their genuine smiles and eagerness to share their culture add an invaluable layer to your travel experience. Engaging with the residents and learning about their way of life bridges the gap between traveler and local, creating connections that often remain etched in memory.

As we conclude this guide to Split, it's important to emphasize that this is merely a glimpse into the city's offerings. Split is a destination that caters to a spectrum of interests, from history and architecture to leisure and adventure. Its beauty lies not only in its iconic landmarks but also in the details—the aroma of freshly baked pastries, the sound of the waves lapping against the shore, and the laughter shared with newfound friends.

So, whether you're a history buff, a beach lover, a culinary connoisseur, or an avid explorer, Split has a place for you within its heart. As you embark on your journey through this captivating city, may you discover its hidden corners, embrace its contrasts, and create memories that will resonate long after your departure. Split beckons, ready to welcome you into its embrace and create a travel experience that is as unique as it is unforgettable.

Printed in Great Britain
by Amazon

45582252R00116